Computer Science: A Very Short Introduction

VERY SHORT INTRODUCTIONS are for anyone wanting a stimulating and accessible way into a new subject. They are written by experts, and have been translated into more than 40 different languages.

The series began in 1995, and now covers a wide variety of topics in every discipline. The VSI library now contains over 450 volumes—a Very Short Introduction to everything from Psychology and Philosophy of Science to American History and Relativity—and continues to grow in every subject area.

Very Short Introductions available now:

Available soon:

For more information visit our website

www.oup.com/vsi/

Subrata Dasgupta

COMPUTER SCIENCE

A Very Short Introduction

OXFORD
UNIVERSITY PRESS

OXFORD
UNIVERSITY PRESS

Great Clarendon Street, Oxford, OX2 6DP,
United Kingdom

Oxford University Press is a department of the University of Oxford.
It furthers the University's objective of excellence in research, scholarship,
and education by publishing worldwide. Oxford is a registered trade mark of
Oxford University Press in the UK and in certain other countries

© Subrata Dasgupta 2016

The moral rights of the author have been asserted

First edition published in 2016

Impression: 1

Published in the United States of America by Oxford University Press
198 Madison Avenue, New York, NY 10016, United States of America

British Library Cataloguing in Publication Data
Data available

Library of Congress Control Number: 2015950971

ISBN 978-0-19-873346-1

Printed in Great Britain by
Ashford Colour Press Ltd, Gosport, Hampshire

To
Anton Rippon

Contents

Preface

The 1960s were tumultuous times, socially and culturally. But tucked away amidst the folds of the Cold War, civil rights activism, anti-war demonstrations, the feminist movement, student revolt, flower-power, sit-ins, and left-radical insurrections—almost unnoticed—a new science came into being on university campuses in the West and even, albeit more tentatively, in some regions of the non-Western world.

This science was centred on a new kind of machine: the electronic digital computer. The technology surrounding this machine was called by a variety of names, most commonly, 'automatic computation', 'automatic computing', or 'information processing'. In the English-speaking world this science was most widely called *computer science*, while in Europe it came to be labelled 'informatique', or 'informatik'.

The *technological idea* of automatic computation—designing and building real machines that would compute with minimal human intervention—can at least be traced back to the obsessive dreams of the English mathematician and intellectual gadfly Charles Babbage in the early 19th century, if not further back. The *mathematical concept* of computing was first studied in the late 1930s by the logicians Alan Turing in England and Alonzo Church in the United States. But the impetus for a proper *empirical science* of computing had to wait until the invention, design, and implementation of the electronic digital computer in the 1940s, just after the end of the Second World War. Even then, there was a gestation period. An autonomous science with a name and an identity of its own only emerged in the 1960s when universities began offering undergraduate and graduate degrees in computer science, and the first generation of formally trained *computer scientists* emerged from the campuses.

Since the advent of the electronic digital computer in 1946, the spectacular growth of the technologies associated with this machine (nowadays called generically 'information technology' or 'IT') and the related cultural and social transformation (expressed in such terms as 'information age', 'information revolution', 'information society') is visible for all to see and experience. Indeed, we are practically engulfed by this techno-social milieu. The *science*—the intellectual discipline—underlying the technology, however, is less visible and certainly less known or understood outside the professional computer science community. Yet computer science surely stands alongside the likes of molecular biology and cognitive science as being amongst the most consequential new sciences of the post-Second World War era. Moreover, there is a certain strangeness to computer science that compels attention and sets it apart from all other sciences.

My intent in this book is to offer the intellectually curious reader seriously interested in scientific ideas and principles the basis for an understanding of the fundamental nature of computer science; to enrich, if you will, the public understanding of this strange, historically unique, highly consequential, and still new, science. Put simply, this book strives to answer in direct, immediate, and concise fashion the question: *What is computer science?*

Before we proceed, some terminological clarity is in order. In this book I will use the word *computing* as a verb to denote a certain kind of activity; *computation* is used as a noun to signify the outcome of computing; *computational* is used as an adjective; *computer* is a noun which will refer to a device, artefact, or system that does computing; *artefact* refers to anything made by humans (or, sometimes, animals); and a *computational artefact* is any artefact that participates in computational work.

Finally, a caveat must be stated. This book begins by accepting the proposition that computer science is indeed a science; that is, it manifests the broad attributes associated with the concept of science, notably, that it entails the systematic blend of empirical, conceptual, mathematical and logical, quantitative and qualitative modes of inquiry into the nature of a certain kind of phenomena. Questioning this assumption is an exercise in the philosophy of science that is beyond the scope of this book. The abiding issue of interest here is the *nature* of computer science *qua* science and, especially, its distinct and distinguishing character.

Acknowledgements

I thank Latha Menon, my editor at OUP for her support and sage advice on this project from its very onset. Her comments on the penultimate version of the book were especially insightful.

Jenny Nugee always responded readily with editorial help and suggestions at various stages of this work. I thank her.

Four anonymous readers of two different drafts of the manuscript offered invaluable suggestions and comments which I took seriously. I am most grateful to them and wish I could acknowledge them by name.

My thanks to Elman Bashar for preparing the illustrations.

Portions of this material were used in an upper-level undergraduate course on 'Computational Thinking' which I have taught on several occasions to non-computer science majors. Their responses have been most helpful in shaping and sharpening the text.

Finally, as always, my thanks to members of my family. In their different ways each continues to provide the sustenance that makes living the life of the mind worthwhile.

List of illustrations

Chapter 1
The 'stuff' of computing

What is computer science? A, now classic, answer was offered in 1967 by three eminent early contributors to the discipline, Alan Perlis, Allen Newell, and Herbert Simon, who stated, quite simply, that computer science is the study of computers and their associated phenomena.

This is a quite straightforward response and I think most computer scientists would accept it as a rough and ready working definition. It centres on the computer itself, and certainly there would be no computer science without the computer. But both computer scientists and the curious layperson may wish to understand more precisely the two key terms in this definition: 'computers' and their 'associated phenomena'.

An automaton called 'computer'

The computer is an *automaton*. In the past this word, coined in the 17th century (plural, 'automata') meant any artefact which, largely driven by its own source of motive power, performed certain repetitive patterns of movement and actions without external influences. Sometimes, these actions imitated those of humans and animals. Ingenious mechanical automata have been devised since pre-Christian antiquity, largely for the amusement of the wealthy, but some were of a very practical nature as, for example, the water clock said to be invented in the 1st century CE by the engineer Hero of Alexandria. The mechanical weight-driven clock invented in 15th-century Italy is a highly successful and lasting descendant of this type of automaton. In the Industrial Revolution of the 18th century, the operation of a pump to remove water from mines motivated by the 'atmospheric' steam engine invented by Thomas Newcomen (in 1713), and later improved by James Watt (in 1765) and others, was another instance of a practical automaton.

Thus, mechanical automata that perform physical actions of one sort or another have a venerable pedigree. Automata that mimic cognitive actions are of far more recent vintage. A notable example is the 'tortoise' robot *Machina Speculatrix* invented by British neurophysiologist W. Grey Walter in the late 1940s to early 1950s. But the automatic electronic digital computer, developed in the second half of the 1940s, marked the birth process of an entirely new genus of automata; for the computer was an artefact designed to simulate and imitate certain kinds of human *thought* processes.

The idea of computing as a way of imitating human thinking—of the computer as a 'thinking machine'—is a profoundly interesting, disturbing, and controversial notion which I will address later in the book, for it is the root of a branch of computer science called *artificial intelligence* (AI). But many computer scientists prefer to be less anthropocentric about their discipline. Some even deny that computing has any similarity at all to autonomous human thinking. Writing in the 1840s, the remarkable English mathematician Ada Augustus, the Countess of Lovelace, an associate of Charles Babbage (see Preface) pointed out that the machine Babbage had conceived (called the Analytical Engine, the first incarnation of what a century later became the modern general purpose digital computer), had no 'pretensions' to initiating tasks on its own. It could only do what it was ordered to do by humans. This sentiment is often repeated by modern sceptics of AI, such as Sir Maurice Wilkes, one of the pioneers of the electronic computer. Writing at the end of the 20th century and echoing Lovelace, he insisted that computers only did what 'they had been written to do'.

So what *is* it that computers *do* which sets them apart from every other kind of artefact, including other sorts of automata? And what makes computer science so distinctive as a scientific discipline?

For the purpose of this chapter, I will treat the computer as a 'black box'. That is, we will more or less ignore the internal structure and workings of computers; those will come later. For the present we will think of the computer as a generic kind of automaton, and consider only *what* it does, not *how* it does what it does.

Computing as information processing

Every discipline that aspires to be 'scientific' is constrained by the fundamental *stuff* it is concerned with. The stuff of physics comprises matter, force, energy, and motion; that of chemistry is atoms and molecules; the stuff of genetics is the gene; and that of civil engineering comprises the forces that keep a physical structure in equilibrium.

A widely held view amongst computer scientists is that the fundamental stuff of computer science is *information*. Thus, the computer is the means by which information is automatically retrieved from the 'environment', stored, processed, or transformed, and released back into the environment. This is why an alternative term for computing is *information processing*; why in Europe computer science is called 'informatique' or 'informatik'; and why the 'United Nations' of computing is called the International Federation for Information Processing (IFIP).

The problem is that despite the founding of IFIP in 1960 (thus giving official international blessing to the concept of information processing), there remains, to this day, a great deal of misunderstanding about what information *is*. It is, as Maurice Wilkes once remarked, an *elusive* thing.

'Meaningless' information

One significant reason for this is the unfortunate fact that the word 'information' was appropriated by communication engineers to mean something very different from its everyday meaning. We usually think of information as telling us something *about* the world. In ordinary language, information is *meaningful*. The statement 'The average winter temperature in country X is 5 degrees Celsius' tells us something about the climate in country X; it gives us information about X. In contrast, in the branch of communication engineering called 'information theory', largely created by American electrical engineer Claude Shannon in 1948, information is simply a commodity transmitted across communication channels such as telegraph wires and telephone lines. In information theory, information is devoid of meaning. The unit of information in information theory is called the *bit* (short for 'binary digit') and a bit has only two values, usually denoted as '0' and '1'. However, in this age of personal computers and laptops, people are more familiar with the concept of the *byte*. One byte consists of eight bits. Since each bit can have one of two values, a byte of information can have 2^8 (= 256) possible values ranging from 00000000 to 11111111. What bits (or bytes) *mean* is of no concern in this sense of 'information'.

In computing, information processing in this meaningless sense is certainly relevant since (as we will see) a physical computer, made out of electronic circuits, magnetic and electromechanical devices, and the like (collectively dubbed 'hardware'), stores, processes, and communicates information as multiples of bits and bytes. In fact, one of the ways in which the capacity and performance of a computational artefact is specified is in terms of bits and bytes. For example, I may buy a laptop with 6 gigabytes of internal memory and 500 gigabytes of external memory ('hardrive'), (where 1 gigabyte = 10^9 bytes); or we may speak of a computer network transmitting information at the rate of 100 megabits/second (where 1 megabit = 10^3 bits).

'Meaningful' (or semantic) information

But the physical computer is (as we will see in Chapter 2) only one kind of computational artefact. Meaningless information is just one kind of information the computer scientist is interested in. The other, more significant (and arguably more interesting), kind is information that has meaning: *semantic* information. Such information connects to the 'real world'—and in this sense corresponds to the everyday use of the word. For example, when I access the Internet through my personal computer, information processing certainly occurs at the physical or 'meaningless' level: bits are transmitted from some remote computer ('server') through the network to my machine. But I am seeking information that is about something, say the biography of a certain person. The resulting text that I read on my screen means something to me. At this level, the computational artefact I am interacting with is a semantic information processing system.

Such information can, of course, be almost anything about the physical, social, or cultural environment, about the past, about thoughts and ideas of other people as expressed by them publicly, and even about one's own thoughts if they happen to be recorded or stored somewhere. What such meaningful information shares with meaningless information, as computer scientist Paul Rosenbloom has noted, is that it must be expressed in some physical medium such as electrical signals, magnetic states, or marks on paper; and that it resolves uncertainty.

Is information *knowledge*?

But consider an item of semantic information such as the biography of an individual. On reading it, I can surely claim to possess *knowledge* about that individual. And this points to the second source of confusion about the concept of information in ordinary language: the conflation of information with knowledge.

The poet T.S. Eliot had no doubt about their distinction. In his play *The Rock* (1934) he famously asked:

> Where is the wisdom we have lost in knowledge?
> Where is the knowledge we have lost in information?

Eliot was clearly implying a hierarchy: that wisdom is superior to knowledge, and knowledge to information.

Computer scientists generally avoid talking about wisdom as being beyond the scope of their purview. But they have also remained somewhat uneasy about distinguishing knowledge from information, at least in some contexts. For example, in AI, a subfield of computer science, a long-standing problem of interest has been knowledge *representation*—how to represent knowledge about the world in computer memory. Another kind of problem they study is how to *make inferences* from a body of knowledge. The kinds of things AI researchers recognize as knowledge include facts ('All men are mortal'), theories ('Evolution by natural selection'), laws ('Every action has an equal and opposite reaction'), beliefs ('There is a God'), rules ('Always come to a dead stop at a stop sign'), and procedures ('how to make seafood gumbo'), etc. But in what way such entities constitute knowledge and not information remains largely unsaid. AI researchers may well claim that what they do, in their branch of computer science, is knowledge processing rather than information processing; but they seem to fall shy of explaining why their concern is knowledge and not information.

In another specialty known as 'data mining' the concern is 'knowledge discovery' from large volumes of data. Some data mining researchers characterize knowledge as 'interesting' and 'useful' patterns or regularities hidden in large databases. They distinguish knowledge discovery from information retrieval (another kind of computing activity) in that the latter is concerned with retrieving 'useful' information from a database on the basis of some query, whereas the former identifies knowledge that is more than just 'useful' information, or more than patterns of regularity: such information must be 'interesting' in some significant sense to become knowledge. Like T.S. Eliot, data mining researchers rate knowledge as superior to information. At any rate, knowledge processing is what data mining is about rather than information retrieval.

Luciano Floridi, a philosopher of computing, offered the following view of the information/knowledge nexus. Information and knowledge bear a 'family resemblance'. They are both meaningful entities but they differ in that information elements are isolated like bricks whereas knowledge relates information elements to one another so that one can produce new inferences by way of the relationships.

To take an example: suppose, while driving, I hear on my car radio that physicists in Geneva have detected a fundamental particle called the Higgs boson. This new fact ('The Higgs boson exists') is certainly a piece of new information for me. I may even think that I have acquired some new knowledge. But this would be an illusion unless I can connect this information with other related items of information about fundamental particles and cosmology. Nor would I be able to judge the significance of this information. Physicists possess an integrated web of facts, theories, laws, etc., about subatomic particles, and about the structure of the universe that enable them to assimilate this new fact and grasp its significance or consequences. They possess the knowledge to do this, while I have merely acquired a new piece of information.

Is information *data*?

In mentioning 'data mining', I have introduced another term of great relevance: *data*. And here is yet another source of ambiguity in our making sense of the information concept, especially in the computer science community.

This ambiguity, indeed confusion, was remarked upon by the computer scientist Donald Knuth as far back as 1966, a time when computer science, emerging as a scientific discipline in its own right, was demanding the invention of new concepts and clarification of old ones. Knuth noted that in science there appeared to be some confusion concerning the terms 'information' and 'data'. When a scientist executes an experiment involving measurement, what is elicited might be any one of four entities: the 'true' values of that which is measured; the values that are actually obtained—approximations to the true values; a representation of the values; and the concepts the scientist teases out by analysing the measurements. The word 'data', Knuth asserted, most appropriately applies to the third of these entities. For Knuth, then, speaking as a computer scientist, data is the *representation* of information obtained by observation or measurement in some precise manner. So, in his view, information precedes data. In practice, the relationship between information and data is as murky as that between information and knowledge. Here, I can only cite a few of the diverse views of this relationship.

For Russell Ackoff, a prominent systems and management scientist, data constitute the outcome of observations; they are representations of objects and events. As for information, Ackoff imagined someone asking some questions *of* data which is then 'processed' (presumably by a human being or a machine) to afford answers, and this latter is information. So according to Ackoff, *contra* Knuth, data precedes information.

For Luciano Floridi, data also precedes information but in a different sense. Data exists, according to Floridi, only when there is an absence of uniformity between two states of a system. As he puts it, a datum (the infrequently used singular of 'data') exists whenever there are two variables, x and y such that $x \neq y$. So, for Floridi, data is a condition which itself has no meaning except that it signifies the presence of difference. When I am approaching a traffic light for instance, my observation of a red signal is a datum because it could have been otherwise: yellow or green.

Given this definition of data, Floridi then defines information as one or more data elements that are structured according to some rules, and are meaningful. To use the linguist's jargon, information is data when it possesses both syntax and semantics. Thus, my observation of the red traffic signal, a datum, becomes information because the meaning of the red light is that 'motorists must stop at the traffic light'. If I did not associate this action with the red light, the latter would remain only a datum.

As a final example, for AI researchers Jeffrey Shrager and Pat Langley, data do not result *from* observation; rather, observation *is* data; more precisely, what is observed is selectively recorded to qualify as data. Information does not figure in their scheme of things.

The programmer's point of view

These examples suffice to demonstrate the murkiness of the information/data connection from different perspectives. But let me return to Knuth. His definition of data reflects to a large extent, I think, the view of those computer scientists who specialize in another aspect of computer science, namely, computer programming—the techniques by which humans communicate a computational task to the computer (a topic I discuss later in this book). Even while paying lip service to the idea of computing as information processing, programmers and programming theorists do not generally reflect on 'information'; rather, they are more concerned with the Knuthian idea of data. More precisely, they concern themselves with data as the fundamental objects ('data objects') upon which computations are performed; and, thus, they are preoccupied with the classification of data objects ('data types'), the rules for representing complex data objects ('data structures'), and the rules for manipulating, processing, and transforming such data objects to produce new data objects. For such computer scientists it is data that matters, not information, not knowledge. To be more exact, programmers take for granted that there is information 'out there' in the 'real world'. But the interesting question for them is how to represent real world information in a form that is appropriate not only for automatic computing but also for human understanding. (Needless to say, other practitioners, such as historians, statisticians, and experimental scientists, do not usually regard data in this fashion.)

I will elaborate on this later in the book. But to give a very simple example of the programmer's view of data: in a university environment there will exist information in the registrar's office about its body of enrolled students: their names, dates of birth, home addresses, email addresses, names of parents or guardians, the subjects they are majoring in, the courses taken, the grades obtained, scholarships held, fees paid, and so on. The university administration needs a system that will organize this information in a systematic fashion (a 'database') such that, perhaps, information concerning any particular student can be accurately and speedily retrieved; new information about existing or new students can be inserted; the progress of individual students can be efficiently tracked; and statistics about the student population as a whole or some subset can be gathered. The programmer given the task of creating such a system is not concerned with the information per se, but rather, given the nature of the information, how to identify the basic data objects representing student information, construct data structures representing the data objects, and build a database so as to facilitate the computational tasks the university administration demands.

Symbol structures as the common denominator

I started this chapter with the proposition that the basic stuff of computing is information; that the computer is an automaton that processes information; and that consequently, computer science is the study of information processing.

But we have also seen that to some computer scientists (such as AI researchers) the fundamental stuff of computing is knowledge rather than information; and to others (such as programmers and programming theorists) it is data rather than information. We get a sense of the varied usages of these three entities from the following sample of terms found in the computing literature (some of which have already appeared in this chapter, others will be found in later ones):

Data type, data object, data structure, database, data processing, data mining, big data...

Information processing, information system, information science, information structure, information organization, information technology, information storage and retrieval, information theory...

Knowledge base, knowledge system, knowledge representation, knowledge structure, theory of knowledge, declarative knowledge, procedural knowledge, knowledge discovery, knowledge engineering, knowledge level...

Can we then reduce these three entities, information, data, knowledge to a common denominator? Indeed we can. Computer scientist Paul Rosenbloom equated information with *symbols*, but we can go further. As far as computer science is concerned, all these three entities can be (and usually are) expressed by symbols—or, rather, by systems of symbols, *symbol structures*—that is, entities that 'stand for', represent, or denote other entities.

Symbols need a medium in which they are expressed, such as marks on paper. For example, the text 'The Higgs boson exists' is a symbol structure whose component symbols are alphabetic characters referring to sound units or phonemes, plus the 'blank' symbol; these when strung together represents something about the physical world. For the physics layperson, this is an item of information; for the particle physicist, this becomes a constituent of her knowledge system concerning fundamental particles. However, the physicist's knowledge which allows her to make sense of this information is itself a far more complex symbol structure stored in her brain and/or printed as text in books and articles. And Knuth's idea of data as the representation of information means that data are also symbol structures representing other symbol structures denoting information. Even the 'meaningless' information of information theory, the bits and bytes, are represented by physical symbols within a computer, such as voltage levels or magnetic states, or on paper by strings of 0s and 1s.

So in its *most* fundamental essence, the stuff of computing is symbol structures. *Computing is symbol processing*. Any automaton capable of processing symbol structures is a computer. The 'phenomena' associated with computers as Perlis, Newell, and Simon suggested are all ultimately reducible to symbol structures and their processing. Computer science is, ultimately, the science of automatic symbol processing, an insight which Allen Newell and Herbert Simon have emphasized. We may choose to call such symbol structures information, data, or knowledge depending on the particular 'culture' within computer science to which we belong.

It is this notion—that computing is ultimately symbol processing; that the computer is a symbol processing automaton; that computer science is the science of symbol processing—which sets computer science apart from other disciplines. As to its strangeness, this will be explained in a later chapter.

Chapter 2
Computational artefacts

We think of *the computer* as the centrepiece of computing; thus, of computer science. And rightly so. But there are caveats to be noted.

First, what exactly constitutes 'the computer' can be debated. Some tend to think of it as the physical object they work with on a daily basis (a laptop or their workplace desktop). Others think of the total system at their disposal, including such facilities as email service, word processing, accessing databases, etc., as 'the computer'. Still others relate it to an entirely mathematical model called the Turing machine (discussed later in this chapter).

Second, accepting that the computer is a symbol processing automaton, there are also other symbol processing artefacts associated with the computer, but which seem slightly at odds with our intuitive idea of 'the computer'. Thus, it behoves us to be more eclectic in our view of artefacts that participate in the computing process; hence the term *computational artefact*. In this chapter we consider the nature of computational artefacts.

In Chapter 1, the computer appeared as (more or less) a black box. All that was said was that it is a symbol processing automaton: it accepts symbol structures (denoting information, data, or knowledge as the case may be) as input and produces (of its own impetus) symbol structures as output.

When we prise open this black box we find that it is rather like a set of nested boxes: inside we find one or more smaller boxes; opening one of these inner boxes reveals still smaller boxes nested within. And so on. Of course, the degree of nesting of black boxes is finite; sooner or later we reach the most primitive boxes.

The natural and artificial worlds both manifest instances of this phenomenon—called *hierarchy*. Many physical, biological, social, and technological systems are hierarchical in structure. The difference between natural hierarchies (as in living systems) and artificial ones (as in cultural or technological systems) is that scientists have to *discover* the former and *invent* the latter.

The modern computer is a hierarchically organized system of computational artefacts. Inventing, understanding, and applying rules and principles of hierarchy is, thus, a subdiscipline of computer science.

There is a reason why hierarchies exist in both natural and artificial domains, and we owe this insight, most notably, to the polymath scientist Herbert Simon. Hierarchical organization, he stated, is a means of managing the *complexity* of an entity. In Simon's language, an entity is complex if it is composed of a number of components that interact in a non-trivial (that is, non-obvious) way. As we will see, the computer manifests this kind of complexity, hence it too is composed as a hierarchical system. The designers and implementers of computer systems are forced to structure them according to principles and rules of hierarchy. Computer scientists have the responsibility of inventing these rules and principles.

Compositional hierarchy

In general, a hierarchical system consists of components partitioned across two or more *levels*. The most common principles of hierarchy are concerned with the relationship of components both within and across levels.

Figure 1 depicts what I will call 'MY-COMPUTER'. (Physically, this may be a desktop, a laptop, a tablet, or even a smart phone. For convenience, I will assume it is one of the first two.) Suppose I use MY-COMPUTER only for three kinds of tasks: to write texts (as I am doing now), to send emails, and to search the (World Wide) Web via the Internet. Thus, I view it as consisting of three *computing tools* which I will call TEXT, MAIL, and WEB-SEARCH (level 1 of Figure 1), respectively. Each is a symbol processing computational artefact. Each is defined (for me as the tool user) in terms of certain *capabilities*. For example, TEXT offers a user-interface allowing me to input a stream of characters, and give commands to align margins, set spacing between lines, paginate, start a new paragraph, indent, insert special symbols, add footnotes and endnotes, italicize and boldface, and so on. It also allows me to input a stream of characters which, using the commands, is set into text which I can save for later use and retrieve.

From my point of view, TEXT *is* MY-COMPUTER when I am writing an article or a book (as at this moment), just as MAIL or WEB-SEARCH *is* MY-COMPUTER when I am emailing or searching the Web, respectively. More precisely, I am afforded three different, alternative *illusions* of what MY-COMPUTER is. Computer scientists refer to such illusionary artefacts as *virtual machines*, and the creation, analysis, and understanding of such virtual machines is one of the major concerns in computer science. They constitute one of the phenomena surrounding computers that Perlis, Newell, and Simon alluded to.

The term *architecture* is used generically by computer scientists to mean the logical or functional structure of computational artefacts. (The term *computer architecture* has a more specialized meaning which will be discussed later.) From my (or any other user's) point of view, the computing tool TEXT has a certain architecture which is visible to me: it has an interpreter that interprets and executes commands; a temporary or working

Legends

▭	Virtual machine	cm	'is composed of'
		cn	'is constructed on'
▭ (Software)	Software	a	abstraction
		r	refinement
⬭	Real machine		

1. **Abstraction and hierarchy inside a computer system.**

16

memory whose content is the text I am composing; a permanent or long-term memory which holds all the different texts as files I have chosen to save; input channels that transmits my character streams and commands to the machine, and output channels that allow the display of texts on a screen or as printed matter ('hardcopy'). These components are 'functional': I may not know (or particularly care) about the actual media in which these components exist. And because they characterize all I (as the user) need to know about TEXT to be able to use it, we will call it TEXT's architecture.

Likewise, when emailing, the tool MAIL *is* MY-COMPUTER: a virtual computational artefact. This too is a symbol processor. It manifests a user-interface that enables me to specify one or more recipients of a message; link one or more other symbol structures (texts, pictures) as attachments that accompany the message; compose the message; and send it to the recipient(s). Its architecture resembles that of TEXT in that it manifests the same kinds of components. It can interpret commands, has an input channel enabling character streams to be assembled in a working memory, a long-term memory to hold, as long as I want, my messages, and output channels for displaying the contents of the email on the screen and printing it out. In addition, MAIL has access to other kinds of long-term memory which hold the symbol structures (texts and images) that can be attached to the message; however, one of these long-term memories is *private* to MY-COMPUTER and so, can only be accessed by me, while the other is *public*—that is, shared with users of other computers.

Finally, there is WEB-SEARCH. Its architecture is similar: an interpreter of the commands; a shared/public memory (the Web) whose contents ('web pages') are accessible; a private working memory that (temporarily) holds the contents accessed from shared memory; a private long-term memory which can save these contents; and input and output channels.

The hierarchy shown in part A of Figure 1 is two-levelled. At the upper level (0) is a single computational artefact, MY-COMPUTER; but the lower level (1) shows that MY-COMPUTER is composed of three independent tools. This lower level constitutes my tool box as it were. This type of hierarchy, when an entity *A* is composed of entities *a, β, γ,...*, is ubiquitous in complex systems of any kind, natural or artificial. It is certainly a characteristic of computational artefacts. There is no commonly accepted term for it, so let us call it *compositional hierarchy*.

Abstraction/refinement

As we have noted, the three computing tools at level 1 of Figure 1 are similar in their respective architectures. Each comprises of shared and private long-term memories, private working memory, input and output channel(s), and interpreter(s) of commands.

But these three computing tools must have been *implemented* for them to be actual working artefacts: For instance, someone must have designed and implemented a computational artefact which when activated *performs* as TEXT, hiding the details of the mechanisms by which TEXT was realized. Let us denote this implemented artefact TEXT* (level 2 of Figure 1); this is a computer program, a piece of software. The relationship between TEXT and TEXT* is one of abstraction/refinement (part B of Figure 1):

> An *abstraction* of an entity *E* is itself another entity *e* that reveals only those characteristics of *E* considered relevant in some context while suppressing other characteristics deemed irrelevant (in that context). Conversely, a *refinement* of an entity *e* is itself another entity *E* such that *E* reveals characteristics that were absent or suppressed in *e*.

TEXT is an abstraction of TEXT*; conversely, TEXT* is a refinement of TEXT. Notice that abstraction/refinement is also a principle of hierarchy in which abstraction is at the upper level and refinement at the lower level. Notice also that abstractions and refinements are context-dependent. The same entity E may be abstracted in different ways to yield two or more higher level entities $e1, e2, \ldots, eN$. Conversely, the same entity e may be refined in two more different ways to yield different lower level entities $E1, E2, \ldots, En$.

The principle of abstraction/refinement as a way of managing the complexity of computational artefacts has a rich history from the earliest years of computing. Perhaps the person who made the emerging computer science community in the 1960s most conscious about the importance of this principle of hierarchy was Edsger Dijkstra. Later we will see its particular importance in the process of *building* computational artefacts, but for the present it is enough for the reader to appreciate how a complex computational artefact can be *understood* in terms of the abstraction/refinement principle, just as a complex computational artefact can be understood in terms of the compositional hierarchy.

Hierarchy by construction

We are no longer 'seeing' MY-COMPUTER from my perspective as a user. We are now in the realm of those who have actually created MY-COMPUTER: the tool builders or artificers. And they are not, incidentally, a homogenous lot.

In particular, TEXT*, MAIL*, and WEB-SEARCH* are computer programs—*software*—which programmers (software developers, as they are now preferably called), have constructed upon an infrastructure which I call here PLINTH (part C and level 3 of Figure 1). This particular infrastructure also consists of a collection of computing tools the builders of TEXT* et al. could use. Here, then, is a third type of hierarchy: *hierarchy by construction*.

Ever since the earliest days of the digital computer, designers and researchers have sought to protect the user, as far as possible, from the gritty, and sometimes nasty, realities of the physical computer, to make the user's life easier. The ambition has always been to create a smooth, pleasant user interface that is close to the user's particular universe of discourse, and remains within the user's comfort zone. A civil or a mechanical engineer wants to perform computations that command the computer to solve the equations of engineering mechanics; a novelist wants his computer to function as a writing instrument; the accountant desires to 'offload' some of her more tedious calculations to the computer; and so on. In each case, the relevant user desires an *illusion* that their computer is tailor-made for his or her need. Much debate has ensued over the years as to whether such user tools and infrastructures should be incorporated into the physical machine ('hardwired') or provided in more flexible fashion by way of software. In general, the partitioning of infrastructures and tools across this divide has been rationalized by the particular needs of the communities for whom computers are developed.

As we have noted, MY-COMPUTER offers such illusions to the user whose sole concerns are typing text, sending and receiving emails, and searching the Web. MY-COMPUTER offers an infrastructure for the user to write texts, compose and send emails, and search for information on the Web, just as PLINTH (at a lower level) offers such an infra-structure for the construction of programs that function as the user's toolkit.

But even the software developers, who created these abstractions by implementing the programs TEXT* et al., must have their own illusions: they too are users of the computer though their engagement with the computer is far more intense than mine when I am using TEXT or MAIL. We may call them 'application programmers' or 'application software developers', and they too must be shielded from some of the realities of the physical computer. They too need an infrastructure *with* which they can work, *upon* which they can create their own virtual machines.

In Figure 1, the entity named PLINTH is such a foundation. It is, in fact, an abstraction of a collection of programs (a 'software system'), shown here as OPSYS* (level 4) which belongs to a class of computational artefacts called *operating systems*.

An operating system is the great facilitator; it is the great protector; it is the great illusionist. In its early days of development, in the 1960s, it was called 'supervisor' or 'executive' and these terms capture well what its responsibilities are. Its function is to manage the resources of the physical computer and provide a uniform set of services to all users of the computer whether layperson or software developer. These services include 'loaders' which will accept programs to be executed and allocating them to appropriate locations in memory; memory management (ensuring that one user program does not encroach upon, or interfere with, the memory used by another program); providing *virtual* memory (giving users the illusion of unlimited memory); controlling physical devices (such as disks, printers, monitors) that perform input and output functions; organizing the storage of information (or data or knowledge) in long-term memories so as to make it easily and speedily accessible; executing procedures according to standardized rules (called 'protocols') that enable a program on one computer to request service from a program in another computer communicated through a network; protecting a user's program from being corrupted by another user's program either accidentally or by the latter user's malice. The infrastructure called PLINTH in Figure 1 provides such services—a set of computing tools; it is an abstraction of the operating system OPSYS*.

Yet, an operating system is not exactly a firewall forbidding all interaction between a program constructed atop it (such as

MAIL*) and the physical computer beneath it. After all, a program will execute by issuing instructions or commands to the physical computer, and most of these instructions will be directly interpreted by the physical computer (in which situation, these instructions are called 'machine instructions'). What the operating system will do is 'let through' machine instructions to the physical computers in a controlled fashion, and interpret other instructions itself (such as those for input and output tasks).

Which brings us to (almost) the bottom of the hierarchy depicted in Figure 1. OPSYS*, the operating system software, is shown here as *constructed*—on top of the physical computer (level 5). For the present we will assume that the physical computer (commonly and crudely called *hardware*) is (finally) the 'real thing'; that there is nothing virtual about it. We will see that this too is an illusion, that the physical computer has its own internal hierarchy and it too has its own levels of abstraction, composition, and construction. But at least we can complete the present discussion on this note: that the physical computer provides an infrastructure and a toolbox comprising a repertoire of instructions (machine instructions), a repertoire of data types (see Chapter 1), modes of organizing and accessing instructions and data in memory, and certain other basic facilities which enable the implementation of programs (especially the operating system) that can be executed by the physical computer.

Three classes of computational artefacts

In a recent book narrating the history of the birth of computer science I commented that a peculiarity of computer science lies in its three classes of computational artefacts.

One class is *material*. These artefacts, like all material objects encountered through history, obey the physical laws of nature (such as Ohm's law, the laws of thermodynamics, Newton's laws of motion, etc.). They consume power, generate heat, entail (in some cases) physical motion, decay physically and chemically over time, occupy physical space, and consume physical time when operational. In our example of Figure 1, the physical computer at level 5 is an instance. Obviously, all kinds of computer hardware are material computational artefacts.

Some computational artefacts, however, are entirely *abstract*. They not only process symbol structures, they *themselves* are symbol structures and are intrinsically devoid of any physicality (though they may be made visible via physical media such as marks on paper or on the computer screen). So physico-chemical laws do not apply to them. They neither occupy physical space nor do they consume physical time. They 'neither toil nor spin' in physical space-time; rather, they exist in their own space-time frame. There are no instances of the abstract artefact in Figure 1. In the next section, I cite examples, and will discuss some of them in chapters to follow. But if you recall the mention of procedures that I as a user of TEXT or MAIL can devise to deploy these tools, such procedures exemplify abstract artefacts.

The third class of computational artefacts are the ones that most lend *strangeness* to computer science. These are abstract *and* material. To be more precise, they are themselves symbol structures, and in this sense they are abstract; yet their operations cause changes in the material world: signals transmitted across communication paths, electromagnetic waves to radiate in space, physical states of devices to change, and so on; moreover, their actions depend on an underlying material agent to execute the actions. Because of this nature, I have called this class *liminal* (meaning a state of ambiguity, of between and betwixt). Computer programs or software is one vast class of liminal computational artefacts, for example, the programs TEXT*, MAIL*, WEB-SEARCH*, and the operating system OPSYS* of Figure 1.

Later, we will encounter another important kind of liminal artefact. For the present, what makes computer science both distinctive and strange is not only the presence of liminal artefacts but also that what we call 'the computer' is a *symbiosis* of the material, the abstract, and the liminal.

Over the approximately six decades during which computer science as an autonomous, scientific discipline evolved, many distinct subclasses of these three classes of computational artefacts have emerged. Four instances—user tool and infrastructure, software, and physical computer—are shown in Figure 1. Of course, some subclasses are more central to computing than others because they are more *universal* in their scope and use than others. Moreover, the classes and subclasses form a compositional hierarchy of their own.

Here is a list of some of these classes and subclasses presently recognized in computer science. The numbering convention demonstrates the hierarchical relationship between them. While the reader may not be familiar with many of these elements, I will explain the most prominent of them in the course of this book.

[1] Abstract artefacts
    [1.1] Algorithms
    [1.2] Abstract automata
        [1.2.1] Turing machines
        [1.2.2] Sequential machines
    [1.3] Metalanguages
    [1.4] Methodologies
    [1.5] Languages
        [1.5.1] Programming languages
        [1.5.2] Hardware description languages
        [1.5.3] Microprogramming languages
[2] Liminal artefacts
    [2.1] User tools and interfaces
    [2.2] Computer architectures
        [2.2.1] Uniprocessor architectures
        [2.2.2] Multiprocessor architectures

The 'great unifier'

There is one computational artefact that must be singled out. This is the *Turing machine*, an abstract machine named after its originator—logician, mathematician, and computer theorist Alan Turing. Let me first describe this artefact and then explain why it deserves special attention.

The Turing machine consists of a tape that is unbounded in length and divided into squares. Each square can hold one of a vocabulary of symbols. At any point in time a read/write head is positioned on one square of the tape which becomes the 'current' square. The symbol in the current square (including the 'empty' symbol or 'blank') is the 'current symbol'. The machine can be in one of a finite number of *states*. The state of the machine at any given time is its 'current state'. Depending on the current symbol and the current state, the read/write head can write (an output) symbol on the current square (overwriting the current symbol), move one square left or right, or effect a change of state, called the 'next state'. The cycle of operation repeats with the next state as the current state, the new current square holding the new current symbol. The relationships between the (possible) current states (CS), (possible) current (input) symbols (I), the (possible) output symbols (O), movements of the read/write head (RW), and the (possible) next states (NS) are specified by a 'state table'. The behaviour of the machine is controlled by the state table and the invisible mechanism that effects the reads and writes, moves the read/write head, and effects changes of state.

Figure 2 depicts a very simple Turing machine which reads an input string of 0s and 1s written on the tape, replaces the input string with 0s except that when the entire string has been scanned, it writes a 1 if the number of 1s in the input string is odd, and 0 otherwise. The machine then comes to a *halt*. A special symbol, say #, on the tape indicates the end of the input string. This machine would be called a 'parity detector': it replaces the entire input string with 0s and replaces # with a 1 or a 0 depending on whether the parity of (the number of 1s in) the input string is odd or even.

This machine needs three states: *So* signifies that an odd number of 1s have been detected in the input string at any point in the machine's operation. *Se* represents the detection of an even number of 1s up to any point in the machine's operation. The third state *H* is the halting state: it causes the machine to halt. When the machine begins operation, its read/write head is pointing to the square holding the first digit in the input string.

The potential behaviour of the Turing machine is specified by the state table (see Table 1).

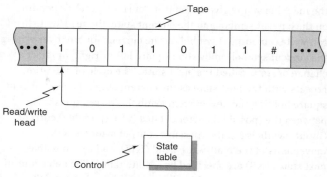

2. General structure of the Turing machine.

Table 1. The state table

Current state	Input symbol	Next state	Output symbol	Move read/ write head
Se	0	*Se*	0	*R*
Se	1	*So*	0	*R*
Se	#	*H*	0	—
So	0	*So*	0	*R*
So	1	*Se*	0	*R*
So	#	*H*	1	—

Each row in this table specifies a distinct operation on the part of the machine and must be interpreted independently. For example, the first row says that: *if* the current state is *Se and* the current input symbol is 0 *then* the next state will (also) be *Se and* output symbol 0 is written on the tape *and* the read/write head is moved one position right. The last row tells us that that *if* the current state is *So and* the input symbol is # *then* replace the # with a 1 *and make* the next state the halt state *H*. There is no further motion of the read/write head.

Suppose the input string is as shown in Figure 2, and the machine is set to the state *Se*. The reader can easily verify that the sequence of states and the contents of the tape in successive cycles of the machine's operation will be as follows. The position of the read/ write head in each cycle is indicated by the asterisk to the right of the 'current' input symbol:

Se: 1*011011# → *So*: 00*11011# → *So*: 001*1011# → *Se*: 0001*011# → *So*: 00000*11# → *So*: 000001*1# → *Se*: 0000001*# → *So*: 0000000#* → *H*: 00000001*

There will be, then, a distinct Turing machine (Turing himself called this, simply, a 'computing machine') for each distinct symbol processing task. Each such (special purpose) Turing machine will specify the alphabet of symbols that the machine will recognize, the set of possible states, the initial square on which the read/write head is positioned, the state table, and the initial current state. At the end of the machine's operation (when it reaches the 'halt' state, if there is one) the output written onto the tape gives the result of the symbol processing task.

Thus, for example, a Turing machine can be built to add two numbers n, m, represented by n 1s followed by a blank followed by m 1s, leaving the result $n + m$ (as a string of $n + m$ 1s) on the tape. Another Turing machine with a single string composed of the symbols a, b, and c as input will replace this input string with a 'mirror image' (called a 'palindrome') of the input string. For example if the input string is '*aaabbbccc*' then the output will be '*cccbbbaaa*'. A Turing machine is, thus, a symbol processing machine. It is, of course, an abstract artefact in the 'purest' sense since the machine itself is a symbol structure. No one would dream of making a physical version of a Turing machine as a *practical* artefact.

But Turing went further. He also showed that one can build a single computing machine **U** that can *simulate* every other Turing machine. If **U** is provided with a tape containing the description of the state table for a specific Turing machine, **U** will interpret that description and perform the same task as that particular machine would do. Such a machine **U** is called a *universal Turing machine*.

The significance of Turing's invention lies in a claim he made that *any procedure that we 'intuitively' or 'naturally' think of as a computing procedure can be realized by a Turing machine*. It follows that a universal Turing machine can perform anything we think of as computing. This claim is called the *Turing thesis* (or sometimes as the Church–Turing thesis, since another logician, Alonzo Church, arrived at the same conclusion using an entirely different line of thinking).

We may think of the Turing machine as the 'great unifier'. It is what binds all computational artefacts; that is, all computational artefacts and their behaviours can be *reduced* to the workings of a Turing machine.

Having said this, and also recognizing that an entire branch of computer science called *automata theory* exists which studies the structure and behaviour, the power and limitations of the Turing machine in all its conceivable manifestations (e.g. in confining the tape to a finite length, or in introducing multiple tapes with multiple read/write heads), we must also recognize the paradoxical situation that the Turing machine has had almost no impact on the invention, design, implementation, and behaviour of any practical (or practicable) computational artefact whatsoever, or on the thinking and practice of computer scientists who deal with such artefacts!

Interactive computing

Moreover, since Turing's time there have emerged computational artefacts that work *interactively* with each other or with other natural or artificial systems. 'Interaction' refers here to the mutual or reciprocal influence amongst artificial (including social) and/or natural *agents* that together form a system of some sort.

Consider, for example, my paying a utilities bill: this entails an interaction between me and my laptop, and my bank's computer system and that of the utility company. In this situation four agents (three computational artefacts and myself) are effecting information transfers and computations interactively, by exchanging messages, commands, and data.

Or consider the abstract computational artefact TEXT in Figure 1. This constitutes a *human–computer interface* whereby the human user of TEXT and the software system TEXT* interact with each other. Commands afforded by TEXT and issued by the user causes

TEXT* to respond (initiating a new line of text, creating a space between words, adding characters to form words in the text, indenting for a new paragraph, italicizing a word, etc.) and this latter response prompts, in turn, the human user to respond.

Such interactive systems do not conform to the 'standard' idea of the Turing machine which is essentially a stand-alone artefact with inputs already inscribed on its tape before the activation of the machine and whose output is only visible when the Turing machine halts. Interactive computational artefacts (such as my bank's or my utility company's system) may never halt.

It is because of such considerations that some computer scientists insist that the study of Turing machines—automata theory—properly belongs to the realm of mathematics and mathematical logic than to computer science proper, while others question the validity of seeing the Turing thesis as encompassing the whole of computing.

Computer science as a science of the artificial

To summarize the discussion so far, computational artefacts are *made* things; they process symbol structures signifying information, data, or knowledge (depending on one's point of view and context). Computer science is the science of computational artefacts.

Clearly, computational artefacts are not part of the natural world in the sense that rocks, minerals and fossils, plants and animals, stars, galaxies and black holes, elementary particles, atoms and molecules are. Human beings bring these artefacts into existence. Thus, computer science is not a *natural* science. So what kind of science is it?

One view is that since computational artefacts are utilitarian, thus technological, computer science is not 'really' a science at all. Rather, it is a branch of engineering. However, the traditional engineering sciences such as strength of materials, theory of structures, thermodynamics, physical metallurgy, circuit theory, as well as such new engineering sciences as bioengineering and genetic engineering are directly constrained by the laws of nature. Liminal and abstract computational artefacts seem a far cry from the uncompromisingly material artefacts—structures, machine tools, engines, integrated circuits, metals, alloys, and composite materials, etc.—studied by engineering scientists. This is one of the reasons why material computational artefacts (computer hardware) often belong to the domain of engineering schools while liminal and abstract ones are in the domain of schools of science.

However, all artefacts—engineering and computational—have something in common: they are the products of human thought, human goals, human needs, human desires. *Artefacts are purposive: they reflect the goals of their creators.*

Herbert Simon called all the sciences concerned with artefacts (abstract, liminal, or material) the *sciences of the artificial*. They stand apart from the natural sciences because they must take into account goals and purposes. A natural object has no purpose: rocks and minerals, stars and galaxies, atoms and molecules, plants and organisms have not come into the world with a purpose. They just *are*. The astronomer does not ask: 'What is a galaxy for?' The geologist does not ask: 'What is the purpose of an igneous intrusion?' The task of the natural scientist is to discover the laws governing the structures and behaviours of natural phenomena, inquire into how they came into being, but not ask why—for what purpose—they came into existence.

In contrast, artefacts have entered the world reflecting human needs and goals. It is not enough to ask what are the laws and principles governing the structure and behaviour of a computational artefact (or, for that matter, of pyramids, suspension bridges, particle accelerators, and kitchen knives) if we then ignore the reason for their existence.

The sciences of the artificial entail the study of the *relationship between means and ends*: the goals or needs for which an artefact is intended, and the artefact made to satisfy the needs. The 'science' in computer science is, thus, a science of means and ends. It asks: given a human need, goal, or purpose, how can a computational artefact *demonstrably* achieve such a purpose? That is, how can one demonstrate, by reason or observation or experiment that the computational artefact satisfies that purpose?

Chapter 3
Algorithmic thinking

Like the character in Molière's play who did not know he had been speaking prose all his life, most people may not realize that, when as children they first multiplied two multi-digit numbers or did long division, they were executing an *algorithm*. Indeed, it is probably the case that before the 1960s few people outside the computing and mathematical communities knew the word 'algorithm'. Since then, however, like 'paradigm' (a term originally made fashionable in the rarified reaches of philosophy of science) 'algorithm' has found its way into common language to mean formulas, rules, recipes, or systematic procedures to solve problems. This is largely due to the intimate association, in the past five decades or so, of computing with algorithms.

Yet, the *concept* of an algorithm (if not the word) reaches back to antiquity. Euclid's great work, *Elements* (*c.*300 BCE) where the principles of plane geometry were laid out, described an algorithm to find the greatest common divisor (GCD) of two positive integers. The word 'algorithm' itself originated in the name of 9th-century Arabic mathematician and astronomer, Mohammed ibn-Musa al-Khwarizmi, who lived and worked in one of the world's premier scientific centres of his age, the House of Wisdom in Baghdad. In one of his many treatises on mathematics and astronomy, al-Khwarizmi wrote on the 'Hindu art of reckoning'. Mistaking this work as al-Khwarizmi's own, later readers of Latin translations called his work 'algorismi' which eventually became 'algorism' to mean a step-by-step procedure. This metamorphosed into 'algorithm'. The earliest reference the *Oxford English Dictionary* could find for this word is in an article published in an English scientific periodical in 1695.

Donald Knuth (who perhaps more than any other person made algorithms part of the computer scientist's consciousness) once described computer science as the study of algorithms. Not all computer scientists would agree with this 'totalizing' sentiment, but none could conceive of a computer science without algorithms at its epicentre. Much like the Darwinian theory of evolution in biology, all roads in computing seem to lead to algorithms. If to think biologically is to think evolutionarily, to think computationally is to form the habit of algorithmic thinking.

The litmus test

As an entry into this realm, consider the *litmus test*, which is one of the first experiments a student performs in high school chemistry.

There is a liquid of some unknown sort in a test tube or beaker. The experimenter dips a strip of blue litmus paper into it. It turns red, therefore the liquid is acidic; it remains blue, it is not acidic. In the latter case the experimenter dips a red litmus strip into the liquid. It turns blue, therefore the liquid is alkaline (basic), otherwise it is neutral.

This is a *decision procedure* chemistry students learn very early in their chemical education, which we can describe in the following fashion:

> **if** a blue litmus strip turns red when dipped into a liquid
> > **then** conclude the liquid is acidic
> > **else**
> > > **if** a red litmus strip turns blue when dipped in the liquid

> **then** conclude the liquid is alkaline
> **else** conclude the liquid is neutral

The notation used here will appear throughout this chapter and in some of the chapters that follow, and needs to be explained. In general, the notation **if** *C* **then** *S1* **else** *S2*, is used in algorithmic thinking to specify decision making of a certain sort. If the condition *C* is true then the *flow of control in the algorithm* goes to the segment *S1*, and *S1* will then 'execute'. If *C* is false then control goes to *S2*, and *S2* will then execute. In either case, after the execution of the **if then else** statement control goes to the statement that follows it in the algorithm.

Notice that the experimenter does not need to know anything about *why* the litmus test works the way it does. She does not need to know what 'litmus' actually is—its chemical composition—nor what chemical process occurs causing the change of colour. To carry out the procedure it is entirely sufficient that (a) the experimenter recognizes litmus paper when she sees it; and (b) she can associate the changes of colour with acids and bases.

The term 'litmus test' has become a metaphor for a definitive condition or test. And for good reasons: it is guaranteed to work. There *will* be an unequivocal outcome; there is no room for uncertainty. Moreover, the litmus test cannot go on indefinitely; the experimenter is assured that within a *finite amount of time* the test will give a decision.

These conjoined properties of the litmus test—a mechanical procedure which is guaranteed to produce a correct result in a finite amount of time—are essential elements characterizing an algorithm.

When is a procedure an algorithm?

For computer scientists, an algorithm is not just a mechanical procedure or a recipe. In order for a procedure to qualify as an algorithm as computer scientists understand this concept, it must possess the following attributes (as first enunciated by Donald Knuth):

Finiteness. An algorithm always terminates (that is, comes to a halt) after a finite number of steps.

Definiteness. Every step of an algorithm must be precisely and unambiguously specified.

Effectiveness. Each operation performed as part of an algorithm must be primitive enough for a human being to perform it exactly (using, say, pencil and paper).

Input and output. An algorithm must have one or more inputs and one or more outputs.

Let us consider Euclid's venerable algorithm mentioned earlier to find the GCD of two positive integers m and n (that is, the largest positive integer that divides exactly into m and n). The algorithm is described here in a language that combines ordinary English, elementary mathematical notation, and some symbols used to signify decisions (as in the litmus test example). In the algorithm, m and n serve as 'input variables' and n also serves as an 'output variable'. In addition, a third 'temporary variable', denoted as r is required. A 'comment', which is not part of the algorithm itself is enclosed in '{ }'. The '←' symbol in the algorithm is of special interest: it signifies the 'assignment operation': '$b ← a$' means to *copy* or *assign* the value of the variable a into b.

Euclid's GCD algorithm. Given two positive integers m and n find their GCD.

Input m, n {m, $n \geq 1$};

Temp var r;

Step 1: divide m by n; $r ←$ remainder; {$0 \leq r \leq$};

Step 2: if $r = 0$ **then Output** n;

　　　　　　　Halt

else

Step 3: $m \leftarrow n$;

   $n \leftarrow r$;

   goto step 1.

Suppose initially $m = 16$, $n = 12$. If a person 'executes' this algorithm using pencil and paper, then the values of the three variables m, n, r after each step's execution will be as follows.

	m	n	r
Step 1:	16	12	4;
Step 3:	12	4	4;
Step 1:	12	4	0;
Step 2:	Output $n = 4$.		

As another example, suppose initially $m = 17$, $n = 14$. The values of the three variables after each step's execution will be the following:

	m	n	r
Step 1:	17	14	3;
Step 3:	14	3	3;
Step 1:	14	3	2;
Step 3:	3	2	2;
Step 1:	3	2	1;
Step 3:	2	1	1;
Step 1:	2	1	0;
Step 2:	Output $n = 1$.		

In the first example, GCD (16, 12) = 4, which is the algorithm's output when it halts; in the second example GCD (17, 14) = 1, which the algorithm outputs after it terminates.

Clearly, the algorithm has inputs. Much less obvious is whether the algorithm satisfies the finiteness criterion. There is a repetition or *iteration* indicated by the **goto** command which causes control to return to step 1. As the two examples indicate, the algorithm iterates between steps 1 and 3 until the condition $r = 0$ is satisfied whereupon the value of n is output as the result and the algorithm comes to a halt. The two examples indicate clearly that for these *particular* pairs of input values for m and n, the algorithm always ultimately satisfies the *termination criterion* ($r = 0$) and will halt. However, how do we know whether for other pairs of values it will not iterate forever alternating steps 1 and 3 and never produces an output? (Thus, in that situation, the algorithm will violate both the finiteness and output criteria.) How do we know that the algorithm will always terminate for all possible positive values of m and n?

The answer is that it must be *demonstrated* that in general, the algorithm is finite. This demonstration lies in that after every test of $r = 0$ in step 2, the value of r is less than the positive integer n, and the values of n and r decreases with every execution of step 1. A decreasing sequence of positive integers must eventually reach 0 and so eventually $r = 0$, and so by virtue of step 2 the procedure will eventually terminate.

What about the definiteness criterion? What this says is that every step of an algorithm must be precisely defined. The actions to be carried out must be unambiguously specified. Thus *language* enters the picture. The description of Euclid's algorithm uses a mix of English and vaguely mathematical notation. The person who mentally executes this algorithm (with the aid of pencil and paper) is supposed to understand exactly what it means to divide, what a remainder is, what positive integers are. He must understand the meaning of the more formal notation, such as the symbols '**if … then … else**', '**goto**'.

As for effectiveness, all the operations to be performed must be primitive enough that they can be done in a finite length of time. In this particular case the operations specified are basic enough that one can carry them out on paper as was done earlier.

'Go forth and multiply'

The concept of *abstraction* applies to the specification of algorithms. In other words, a particular problem may be solved by algorithms specified at two or more different levels of abstraction.

Before the advent of pocket calculators children were taught to multiply using pencil and paper. The following is what I was taught as a child. For simplicity, assume a three-digit number (the 'multiplicand') is being multiplied by a two-digit number (the 'multiplier').

> **Step 1**: Place the numbers so that the multiplicand is the top row and the multiplier is the row below and position them so that the units digit of the multiplier is aligned exactly below the units digit of the multiplicand.
>
> **Step 2**: Draw a horizontal line below the multiplier.
>
> **Step 3**: Multiply the multiplicand by the units digit of the multiplier and write the result ('partial product') below the horizontal line, positioning it so that the units digits are all aligned.
>
> **Step 4**: Place a '0' below the units digit of the partial product obtained in step 3.
>
> **Step 5**: Multiply the multiplicand with the tens digit of the multiplier and position the result (partial product) on the second row below the horizontal line to the left of the '0'.
>
> **Step 6**: Draw another horizontal line below the second partial product.
>
> **Step 7**: Add the two partial products and write it below the second horizontal line.
>
> **Step 8**: Stop. The number below the second line is the desired result.

Notice that to perform this procedure successfully the child has to have *some* prior knowledge: (a) She must know how to multiply a multi-digit number by a one-digit number. This entails either memorizing the multiplication table for two one-digit multiplications or having access to the table. (b) She must know how to add two or more one-digit numbers; and she must know how to handle carries. (c) She must know how to add two multi-digit numbers.

However, the child does *not* need to know or understand *why* the two numbers are aligned according to step 1; or *why* the second partial product is shifted one position to the left as per step 5; or *why* a '0' is inserted in step 4; or *why* when she added the two partial products in step 7 the correct result obtains.

Notice, though, the preciseness of the steps. As long as someone follows the steps exactly as stated this procedure is guaranteed to work provided conditions (a) and (b) mentioned earlier are met by the person executing the procedure. It is guaranteed to produce a correct result in a finite amount of time: the fundamental characteristics of an algorithm.

Consider how most of us nowadays would do this multiplication. We will summon our pocket calculator (or smart phone), and we will proceed to use the calculator as follows:

> **Step 1'**: Enter the multiplicand.
> **Step 2'**: Press 'x'.
> **Step 3'**: Enter the multiplier.
> **Step 4'**: Press '='.
> **Step 5'**: Stop. The result is what is displayed.

This is also a multiplication algorithm. The two algorithms achieve the same result but they are at two different levels of abstraction. Exactly what happens in executing steps 1'–4' in the second algorithm the user does not know. It is quite possible that the calculator is *implementing* the same algorithm as the paper and pencil version. It is equally possible that a different implementation is used. This information is hidden from the user.

The levels of abstraction in this example also imply levels of *ignorance*. The child using the paper-and-pencil algorithm knows *more* about multiplication than the person using a pocket calculator.

The determinacy of algorithms

An algorithm has the comforting property that its performance does not depend on the performer, as long as the knowledge conditions (a)–(c) mentioned earlier are satisfied by the performer. For the same input to an algorithm the same output will obtain regardless of who (or what) is executing the algorithm. Moreover, an algorithm will always produce the same result regardless of when it is executed. Collectively, these two attributes imply that algorithms are *determinate*.

Which is why cookbook recipes are usually not algorithms: oftentimes they include steps that are ambiguous, thus undermining the definiteness criterion. For example, they may include instructions to add ingredients that have been 'mashed lightly' or 'finely grated' or an injunction to 'cook slowly'. These instructions are too ambiguous to satisfy the conditions of algorithm-hood. Rather, it is left to the cook's intuition, experience, and judgement to interpret such instructions. This is why the same dish prepared from the same recipe by two different cooks may differ in taste; or why the same recipe followed by the same person on two different occasions may differ in taste. Recipes violate the principle of determinacy.

Algorithms are abstract artefacts

An algorithm is undoubtedly an artefact; it is designed or invented by human beings in response to goals or needs. And insofar as they process symbol structures (as in the cases of the GCD and multiplication algorithms) they are computational. (Not all algorithms process symbol structures: the litmus test takes physical entities—a test tube of liquid, a litmus strip—as inputs and produces a physical state—the colour of the litmus strip—as output. The litmus test is a manual algorithm that operates upon physico-chemical entities, not symbol structures; we should not, then, think of it as a computational artefact.)

But algorithms, whether computational or not, themselves have no physical existence. One can neither touch nor hold them, feel them, taste them, or hear them. They obey neither the laws of physics and chemistry nor the laws of engineering sciences. They are *abstract artefacts*. They are made of symbol structures which, like all symbol structures, represent other things in the world which themselves may be physical (litmus paper, chemicals, buttons on a pocket calculator, etc.) or abstract (integers, operations on integers, relations such as equality, etc.).

An algorithm is a tool. And as in the case of most tools, the less the user needs to know its theoretical underpinnings the more effective an algorithm is for the user.

This raises the following point: as an artefact an algorithm is Janus-faced. (Janus was the Roman god of gates who looked simultaneously in two opposite directions.) Its *design* or *invention* generally demands creativity, but its *use* is a purely mechanical act demanding little creative thought. Executing an algorithm is, so to speak, a form of mindless thinking.

Algorithms are *procedural knowledge*

As artefacts, algorithms are tools users deploy to solve problems. Once created and made public they belong to the world. This is what makes algorithms objective (as well as determinate) artefacts. But algorithms are also embodiments of knowledge. And being objective artefacts they are embodiments of what philosopher of science Karl Popper called 'objective knowledge'. (It may sound paradoxical to say that the user of an algorithm is both a 'mindless thinker' yet a 'knowing subject'; but even thinking mindlessly is still thinking, and thinking entails drawing upon knowledge of some sort.) But what *kind* of knowledge does the algorithm represent?

In the natural sciences we learn definitions, facts, theories, laws, etc. Here are some examples from elementary physics and chemistry.

(i) The velocity of light in a vacuum is 186,000 miles per second.

(ii) Acceleration is the rate of change of velocity.

(iii) The atomic weight of hydrogen is 1.

(iv) There are four states of matter, solid, liquid, gas, and plasma.

(v) When the chemical elements are arranged in order of atomic numbers there is a periodic (recurring) pattern of the properties of the elements.

(vi) Combustion requires the presence of oxygen.

In each case something is *declared* to be the case: that combustion requires the presence of oxygen; that the atomic weight of hydrogen is 1; that acceleration is the rate of change of velocity; and so on. The (approximation to) truth of these statements is either by way of definition (ii); calculation (i); experimentation or observation (iv, vi); or reasoning (v). Strictly speaking, taken in isolation, they are items of information which when assimilated become part of a person's knowledge (see Chapter 1). This kind of knowledge is called *declarative knowledge* or, more colloquially, 'know-that' knowledge.

Mathematics also has declarative knowledge, in the form of definitions, axioms, or theorems. For example, a fundamental axiom of arithmetic, due to the Italian mathematician Giuseppe Peano is the principle of mathematical induction:

> Any property belonging to zero, and also to the immediate successor of every number that has that property, belongs to all numbers.

Pythagoras's theorem, in contrast, is a piece of declarative knowledge in plane geometry by way of reasoning (by proof):

> In a right-angled triangle with sides a, b forming the right angle and c the hypotenuse, the relationship $c^2 = a^2 + b^2$ is true.

Here is an example of declarative mathematical knowledge by definition:

The *factorial* of a non-negative integer n is:

$$\text{factorial } (n) = 1 \text{ for } n = 0 \text{ or } n = 1$$
$$= n \, (n-1)(n-2)\ldots3.2.1 \text{ for } n > 1$$

In contrast, an algorithm is not declarative; rather it constitutes a procedure, describing how to do something. It prescribes action of some sort. Accordingly, an algorithm is an instance of *procedural knowledge* or, colloquially, 'know-how'.

For a computer scientist it is not enough to know that the factorial of a number is defined as such and such. She wants to know *how to compute* the factorial of a number. She wants an algorithm, in other words. For example:

FACTORIAL
      Input: $n \geq 0$;
      Temp variable: *fact*;
      Step 1: *fact* ← 1;
      Step 2: **if** $n \neq 0$ **and** $n \neq 1$ **then**
            repeat
      Step 3: *fact* ← *fact* * n;
      Step 4: $n = n - 1$;
      Step 5: **until** $n = 1$;
      Step 6: output *fact*;
      Step 7: halt

The notation **repeat** S **until** C specifies an *iteration* or *loop*. The statement(s) S will iteratively execute until the condition C is true. When this happens, the loop terminates and control flows to the statement following the iteration.

Here, in step 1, *fact* is assigned the value 1. If $n = 0$ or 1, then the condition in step 2 is not satisfied, in which case control goes directly to step 6 and the value of *fact* = 1 is output and the algorithm halts in step 7. On the other hand if n is neither 1 nor 0 then the *loop* indicated by the **repeat...until** segment is iteratively executed, each time decrementing n by 1 until the loop *termination* condition $n = 1$ is satisfied. Control then goes to step 6 which when executed outputs the value of *fact* as $n(n-1)(n-2)\ldots3.2.1$.

Notice that the same concept—'factorial'—can be presented both declaratively (as mathematicians would prefer) and procedurally (as computer scientists would desire). In fact the declarative form provides the underlying 'theory' ('what is a factorial?') for the procedural form, the algorithm ('how do we compute it?').

In summary, algorithms constitute a form of procedural but objective knowledge.

Designing algorithms

The abstractness of algorithms has a curious consequence when we consider the *design* of algorithms. This is because, in general, design is a goal-oriented (purposive) act which begins with a set of requirements R to be met by an artefact A yet to exist, and ends with a symbol structure that represents the desired artefact. In the usual case this symbol structure is *the design D(A)* of the artefact A. And the designer's goal is to create D(A) such that if A is implemented according to D(A) then A will satisfy R.

This scenario is unproblematic when the artefact A is a material one; the design of a bridge, for example, will be a representation of the structure of the bridge in the form of engineering drawings and a body of calculations and diagrams showing the forces operating on the structure. In the case of algorithms as artefacts, however, the artefact itself is a symbol structure. Thus, to speak of the design of an algorithm is to speak of a symbol structure (the design) representing another symbol structure (the algorithm). This is somewhat perplexing.

So in the case of algorithms it is more sensible and rational to think of the design and the artefact as the same. The task of designing an algorithm is that of creating a symbol structure which *is* the algorithm A such that A satisfies the requirements R.

The operative word here is 'creating'. Designing is a creative act and, as creativity researchers have shown, the creative act is a complicated blend of reason, logic, intuition, knowledge, judgement, guile, and serendipity. And yet design theorists do talk about a 'science of design' or a 'logic of design'.

Is there, then a scientific component to the design of algorithms? The answer is: 'up to a point'. There are essentially three ways in which a 'scientific approach' enters into the design of algorithms.

To begin with, a design problem does not exist in a vacuum. It is contextualized by a body of knowledge (call it a 'knowledge space') relevant to the problem and possessed by the designer. In designing a new algorithm this knowledge space becomes relevant. For instance, a similarity between the problem at hand and the problem solved by an existing algorithm (which is part of the knowledge space) may be discovered; thus the technique applied in the latter may be transferred to the present problem. This is a case of *analogical reasoning*. Or a known design strategy may seem especially appropriate to the problem at hand, so this strategy may be attempted, though with no guarantee of its success. This is a case of *heuristic reasoning*. Or there may exist a formal theory relevant to the domain to which the problem belongs; thus the theory may be brought to bear on the problem. This is a case of *theoretical reasoning*.

In other words, forms of reasoning may be brought to bear in designing an algorithm based on a body of established or well-tried or proven knowledge (both declarative and procedural). Let us call this the *knowledge factor* in algorithm design.

But, just to come up with an algorithm is not enough. There is also the obligation to convince oneself and others that the algorithm is *valid*. This entails demonstrating by systematic reasoning that the algorithm satisfies the original requirements. I will call this the *validity factor* in algorithm design.

Finally, even if it is shown that the algorithm is valid this may not be enough. There is the question about its performance: how *good* is the algorithm? Let us call this the *performance factor* in algorithm design.

These three 'factors' all entail the kinds of reasoning, logic, and rules of evidence we normally associate with science. Let us see by way of some examples how they contribute to the science of algorithm design.

The problem of translating arithmetic expressions

There is a class of computer programs called *compilers* whose job is to translate a program written in a 'high level' programming language (that is, a language that abstracts from the features of actual physical computers; for example, Fortran or C++) into a sequence of instructions that can be directly executed (interpreted) by a specific physical computer. Such a sequence of machine-specific instructions is called 'machine code'. (Programming languages are discussed in Chapter 4.)

A classical problem faced by the earliest compiler writers (in the late 1950s and 1960s) was to develop algorithms to translate *arithmetic expressions* that appear in the program into machine code. An example of such an expression is

$$(a+b)*(c-1/d)$$

Here, +, −, *, and / are the four arithmetic operators; variables a, b, c, d and the constant number 1 are called 'operands'. An expression of this form, in which the arithmetic operators appear between its two operands is called an 'infix expression'.

The knowledge space surrounding this problem (and possessed by the algorithm designer) includes the following *rules of precedence* of the arithmetic operators:

1. In the absence of parentheses, *, / have precedence over +, −.
2. *, / have the same precedence; +, − have the same precedence.
3. If operators of the same precedence appear in an expression, then left-to-right precedence applies. That is, operators are applied to operands in order of their left-to-right occurrence.
4. Expressions within parentheses have the highest precedence.

Thus, for example in the case of the expression given earlier, the order of operators will be:

a. Perform $a+b$. Call the result $t1$.
b. Perform $1/d$. Call the result $t2$.
c. Perform $c-t2$. Call the result $t3$.
d. Perform $t1*t3$.

On the other hand if the expression was parenthesis-free:

$$a+b*c-1/d$$

then the order of operators would be:

i.   Perform $b * c$. Call the result $t1'$.
ii. Perform $1/d$. Call the result $t2'$.
iii. Perform $a + t1'$. Call the result $t3'$.
iv. Perform $t3' - t2'$.

An algorithm can be designed to produce machine code which when executed will correctly evaluate infix arithmetic expressions according to the precedence rules. (The precise nature of the algorithm will depend on the nature of the machine-dependent instructions, an idiosyncracy of the specific physical computer.) Thus the algorithm, based on the precedence rules, draws on precise rules that are part of the knowledge space relevant to the problem. Moreover, because the algorithm is based directly on the precedence rules, arguing for the algorithm's validity will be greatly facilitated. However, as the earlier examples show, parentheses make the translation of an infix expression somewhat more complicated.

There is a notation for specifying arithmetic expressions without the need for parentheses, invented by the Polish logician Jan Lukasiewiz (1878–1956) and known, consequently, as 'Polish notation'. In one form of this notation, called 'reverse Polish', the operator immediately follows its two operands in a reverse Polish expression. The following examples show the reverse Polish form for a few infix expressions.

a.   For $a + b$ the reverse Polish is $a\ b\ +$.
b.   For $a + b - c$ the reverse Polish is $a\ b\ +\ c\ -$.
c.   For $a + b * c$ the reverse Polish is $a\ b\ c\ *\ +$.
d.   For $(a + b) * c$ the reverse Polish is $a\ b\ +\ c\ *$.

The evaluation of a reverse Polish expression proceeds left-to-right in a straightforward fashion, thus making the translation problem easier. The rule is that the arithmetic operators encountered are applied to their preceding operands in the order of the appearance of the operators, left-to-right. For example, in the case of the infix expression

$$(a + b) * (c-1/d)$$

the reverse Polish form is

$$ab + c1d/ - *$$

and the order of evaluation is:

i. Perform $a\ b$ + and call the result $t1$. So the resulting expression is $t1\ c\ 1\ d/ - *$.

ii. Perform $1\ d/$ and call the result $t2$. So the resulting expression is $t1\ c\ t2 - *$.

iii. Perform $c\ t2$ – and call the result $t3$. So the resulting expression is $t1\ t3\ *$.

iv. Perform $t1\ t3\ *$.

Of course, programmers will write arithmetic expressions in the familiar infix form. The compiler will implement an algorithm that will first translate infix expressions into reverse Polish form and then generate machine code from the reverse Polish expressions.

The problem of converting infix expressions to reverse Polish form illustrates how a sound theoretical basis and a proven design strategy can combine in designing an algorithm that is provably correct.

The design strategy is called *recursion*, and is a special case of a broader problem solving strategy known as 'divide-and-rule'. In the latter, given a problem *P*, if it can be partitioned into smaller subproblems *p1, p2,…, pn*, then solve *p1, p2,…, pn* independently and then combine the solutions to the subproblems to obtain a solution for *P*.

In recursion, the problem *P* is divided into a number of subproblems *that are of the same type as P but smaller*. Each subproblem is divided into still smaller subproblems of the same type and so on until the subproblems become small and simple enough to be solved directly. The solutions of the subproblems are then combined to give solutions to the 'parent' subproblems, and these combined to form solutions to *their* parents until a solution to the original problem *P* obtains.

Consider now the problem of converting algorithmically infix expressions into reverse Polish expressions. Its basis is a set of formal rules:

Let $B = \{+, -, *, /\}$ be the set of binary arithmetic operators (that is, each operator *b* in *B* has exactly two operands). Let *a* denote an operand. For an infix expression *I* denote by *I'* its reverse Polish form. Then:

(a) If *I* is a single operand *a* the reverse Polish form is *a*.

(b) If *I1 b I2* is an infix expression where *b* is an element of *B*, then the corresponding reverse Polish expression is *I1' I2' b*.

(c) If (*I*) is an infix expression its reverse Polish form is *I'*.

The recursive algorithm constructed directly from these rules is shown later as a *function*—in the mathematical sense of this term. In mathematics, a function *F applied* to an 'argument' *x*, denoted *Fx* or *F(x)*, returns the value of the function for *x*. For example, the trigonmetric function SIN applied to the argument 90 (degrees), denoted as SIN 90, returns the value 1. The square root function symbolized as $\sqrt{}$ applied to an argument, say 4 (symbolized as $\sqrt{4}$), returns the value 2.

Accordingly, the algorithm, named here RP with an infix expression I as argument is as follows.

RP (I)

Step 1:   **if** $I = a$ **then** return a

                     else

Step 2:   **if** $I = I1\ b\ I2$

                             then return RP ($I1$) RP ($I2$) b

                         else

Step 3:   **if** $I = (I1)$ **then** return RP ($I1$)

Step 4:   halt

Step 3, of the general form **if** C **then** S is a special case of the **if then else** decision form: control flows to S only if condition C is true, otherwise control flows to the statement that follows the **if then**.

The function RP can thus activate *itself* recursively with 'smaller' arguments. It is easily seen that RP is a direct implementation of the conversion rules and so, is correct by construction. (Of course, not all algorithms are so self-evidently correct; their theoretical foundation may be much more complex and their correctness must then be demonstrated by careful argument or even some form of mathematical proof; or their theoretical basis may be weak or even non-existent.)

To illustrate how the algorithm works with actual arguments, consider the following examples.

(a) Suppose $I = a + b$. Then:

    RP ($a + b$) = RP (a) RP (b) +   (by step 2)

                = ab+   (by step 1 twice)

(b) Suppose $I = (a + b) * c$. Then:

    RP (($a + b$) * c) = RP ($a + b$) RP (c) *   (by step 2)

                = RP (a) RP (b) + RP (c) *   (by step 2)

                = ab+c*   (by step 1 thrice)

(C) Suppose $I = (a * b) + (c - 1/d)$. Then:

$$RP\, ((a * b) + (c - 1/d))$$
$$= RP\, (a * b)\, RP\, (c - 1/d)\, + \qquad \text{(by step 2)}$$
$$= RP\, (a)\, RP\, (b) * RP\, (c)\, RP\, (1/d)\, - + \qquad \text{(by step 2 thrice)}$$
$$= RP\, (a)\, RP\, (b) * RP\, (c)\, RP\, (1)\, RP\, (d)/ - + \qquad \text{(by step 2)}$$
$$= ab*c1d/ - + \qquad \text{(by step 1 five times)}$$

The 'goodness' of algorithms as utilitarian artefacts

As mentioned before, it is not enough to design a correct algorithm. Like the designer of any utilitarian artefact the algorithm designer must be concerned with how *good* the algorithm is, how efficiently it does its job. Can we *measure* the goodness of an algorithm in this sense? Can we compare two rival algorithms for the same task in some quantitative fashion?

The obvious factor of goodness will be the amount of *time* the algorithm takes to execute. But an algorithm is an abstract artefact. We cannot measure it in physical time; we cannot measure time on a real clock since an algorithm *qua* algorithm does not involve any material thing. If I as a human being execute an algorithm I suppose I could measure the amount of time I take to perform the algorithm mentally (perhaps with the aid of pencil and paper). But that is only a measure of *my* performance of the algorithm on a specific set of input data. Our concern is to measure the performance of an algorithm across all its possible inputs and regardless of who is executing the algorithm.

Algorithm designers, instead, assume that each basic step of the algorithm takes the same unit of time. Think of this as 'abstract time'. And they conceive the *size* of a problem for which the algorithm is designed in terms of the number of data items that the problem is concerned with. They then adopt two measures of algorithmic 'goodness'. One has to do with the *worst case* performance of the algorithm as a function of the size n of the problem; the other measure deals with its *average* performance, again, as a function of the problem size n. Collectively, they are called *time complexity*. (An alternative measure is the *space* complexity: the amount of (abstract) memory space required to execute the algorithm.)

The average time complexity is the more realistic goodness measure, but it demands the use of probabilities and is, thus, more difficult to analyse. In this discussion we will deal only with the worst case scenario.

Consider the following problem. I have a list of n items. Each item consists of a student name and his/her email address. The list is ordered alphabetically by name. My problem is to search the list and find the email address for a particular given name.

The simplest way to do this is to start at the beginning of the list, compare each name part of each item with the given student name, proceed along the list one by one until a match is found, and then output the corresponding email address. (For simplicity, we will assume that the student's given name is somewhere in the list.) We call this the 'linear search algorithm'.

LINEAR SEARCH

Input: *student:* an array of n entries, each entry consisting of two 'fields', denoting *name* (a character string) and *email* (a character string) respectively. For the i-th entry in *student*, denote the respective fields by *student [i].name* and *student[i].email*.

Input: *given-name:* the name being 'looked up'.

Temp variable i: an integer

Step 1: $i \leftarrow 1$;
Step 2:   **while** *given-name* $\neq$ *student[i].name*
Step 3:   **do** $i \leftarrow I + 1$;
Step 4:   output *student[i].email*
Step 5:   halt

Here, the generic notation **while** C **do** S specifies another form of iteration: while the condition C is true repeatedly execute the statement ('loop body') S. In contrast to the **repeat** S **until** C, the loop condition is tested before the loop body is entered on each iteration.

In the worst possible case the desired answer appears in the very last (n-th) entry. So, in the worst case scenario, the **while** loop will be iterated n times. In this problem n, the number of students in the list, is the critical factor: this is the problem size.

Suppose each step takes roughly the same amount of time. In the worst case, this algorithm needs $2n + 3$ time steps to find a match. Suppose n is *very* large (say 20,000). In that case, the additional factor '3' is negligible and can be ignored. The multiplicative factor '2' though doubling n is a constant factor. What dominates is n, the problem size; it is this that might vary from one student list to another. We are interested, then, in saying something about the goodness of the algorithm in terms of the amount of (abstract) time needed to perform the algorithm as a function of this n.

If an algorithm processes a problem of size n in time kn, where k is a constant, we say that the time complexity is *of order n*, denoted as $\mathbf{O}(n)$. This called the *Big O* notation, introduced by a German mathematician P. Bachmann in 1892. This notation gives us a way of specifying the efficiency (complexity) of an algorithm as a function of the problem size. In the case of the linear search algorithm, its worst case complexity in $\mathbf{O}(n)$. If an algorithm solves a problem in the worst case in time kn^2, its worst case time complexity is $\mathbf{O}(n^2)$. If an algorithm takes time k$n$log$n$ its time complexity is $\mathbf{O}(n\log n)$, and so on.

Clearly, then, for the same problem of size n an $\mathbf{O}(\log n)$ algorithm will need less time than an $\mathbf{O}(n)$ algorithm, which will need less time than an $\mathbf{O}(n\log n)$ algorithm, and the latter will need less time than an $\mathbf{O}(n^2)$ algorithm; the latter will be better than an $\mathbf{O}(n^3)$

algorithm. The worst algorithms are those whose time complexity is an *exponential* function of n, such as an $O(2^n)$ algorithm. The differences in the goodness of algorithms with these kinds of time complexities, were starkly illustrated by computer scientists Alfred Aho, John Hopcroft, and Jeffrey Ullman in their influential text *The Design and Analysis of Algorithms* (1974). They showed that, assuming a certain amount of physical time to perform steps of an algorithm, in 1 minute an $O(n)$ algorithm could solve problems of size $n = 6 * 10^4$; an $O(n\log n)$ algorithm for the same problem could solve problems of size $n = 4{,}893$; an $O(n^3)$ algorithm solves the same problem but only of size $n = 39$; and an exponential algorithm of $O(2^n)$ could only solve the problem of size $n = 15$.

Algorithms can thus be placed in a hierarchy based on their Big O time complexity, with an $O(k)$ algorithm (where k is a constant) highest in the hierarchy and exponential algorithms of $O(k^n)$ lowest. Their goodness drops markedly as one proceeds down the hierarchy.

Consider the student list search problem, but this time taking into account the fact that the entries in the list are alphabetically ordered by student name. In this one can do what we *approximately* do when searching a phone book or consulting a dictionary. When we look up a directory we don't start from page one and look up each name one at a time. Instead, supposing the word whose meaning we seek in a dictionary begins with a K. We flip the pages of the dictionary to one that is roughly near the Ks. If we open the dictionary to the Ms, for example, we know we have to flip back; if we open at the Hs we have to flip forward. Taking advantage of the alphabetic ordering we *reduce* the amount of search.

This approach can be followed more exactly by way of an algorithm called *binary search*. Assuming the list has $k = 2^n - 1$ entries, in each step the middle entry is identified. If the student name so identified is alphabetically 'lower' than the given name, the algorithm will ignore the entries to the left of the middle element. It will then identify the middle entry of the right half of the list and again compare. Each time, if the name is not found, it will halve the list again and continue until a match is found.

Suppose that the list has k = 15 (i.e. $2^4 - 1$) entries. And suppose these are numbered 1 through 15. Then it can easily be confirmed that the maximum paths the algorithm will travel will be one of the following:

$8 \rightarrow 4 \rightarrow 2 \rightarrow 1$
$8 \rightarrow 4 \rightarrow 2 \rightarrow 3$
$8 \rightarrow 4 \rightarrow 6 \rightarrow 5$
$8 \rightarrow 4 - \rightarrow 6 \rightarrow 7$
$8 \rightarrow 12 \rightarrow 10 \rightarrow 9$
$8 \rightarrow 12 \rightarrow 10 \rightarrow 11$
$8 \rightarrow 12 \rightarrow 14 \rightarrow 13$
$8 \rightarrow 12 \rightarrow 14 \rightarrow 15$

Here, the list entry 8 is the middle entry. So, at most only $4 = \log_2 16$ entries will be searched before a match is found. For a list of size n the worst case performance of binary search is **O** ($\log n$), an improvement over the linear search algorithm.

The aesthetics of algorithms

The *aesthetic experience*—the quest for beauty—is found not only in art, music, film, and literature but also in science, mathematics, and even technology. 'Beauty is truth, truth beauty', began the final lines of John Keats's *Ode on a Grecian Urn* (1820). The English mathematician G.H. Hardy, echoing Keats, roundly rejected the very idea of 'ugly mathematics'.

Consider why mathematicians seek different proofs for some particular theorem. Once someone has discovered a proof for a theorem why should one bother to find another, different, proof?

The answer is that mathematicians seek new proofs of theorems when the existing ones are aesthetically unappealing. They seek beauty in their mathematics.

This applies just as much to the design of algorithms. A given problem may be solved by an algorithm which is, in some way, *ugly*—that is, clumsy, or plodding. Sometimes this is manifested in the algorithm being inefficient. So computer scientists, especially those who have a training in mathematics, seek beauty in algorithms in exactly the same sense that mathematicians seek beauty in their proofs. Perhaps the most eloquent spokespersons for an aesthetics of algorithms were the computer scientists Edsger Dijkstra from the Netherlands, C.A.R. Hoare from Britain, and Donald Knuth from the United States. As Dijkstra once put it, 'Beauty is our business'.

This aesthetic desire may be satisfied by seeking algorithms being simpler, more well structured, or using a 'deep' concept.

Consider, for example, the factorial algorithm described earlier in this chapter. This iterative algorithm was based on the definition of the factorial function as:

$$\text{fact } (n) = 1 \text{ for } n = 1 \text{ or } n = 0$$
$$= n \, (n-1)(n-2)\ldots3.2.1 \text{ for } n > 1$$

But there is a recursive definition of the factorial function:

$$\text{fact } (n) = 1 \text{ for } n = 1 \text{ or } n = 0$$
$$= n * \text{fact } (n-1) \text{ for } n > 1$$

The corresponding algorithm, as a function, is:

rec-fact (n)
    if $n = 0$ **or** $n = 1$
        then return 1
        else return $n * $ rec-fact $(n-1)$

Many computer scientists would find this a more aesthetically appealing algorithm because of its clean, easily understandable, austere form and the fact that it takes advantage of the more subtle recursive definition of the factorial function. Notice that the recursive and the non-recursive (iterative) algorithms are at different levels of abstraction: the recursive version might be implemented by some variant of the non-recursive version.

Intractable ('really difficult') problems

I end this chapter by shifting focus from algorithms that solve computational problems to the computational problems themselves. In an earlier section we saw that the performance of algorithms can be estimated in terms of their time (or space) complexity. For example, in the case of the student list search problem the two algorithms (linear search and binary search), though solving the same *problem* manifested two different worst case time complexities.

But consider the so-called 'travelling salesman problem': Given a set of cities and road distances between them, can a salesman beginning at his base city visit all the cities and return to his origin such that the total distance travelled is less than or equal to some particular value? As it happens, there is no known algorithm for this problem that is less than of exponential time complexity ($O(k^n)$, for some constant k and problem size n (such as the number of cities)).

A computational problem is said to be *intractable*—'really difficult'—if all the known algorithms to solve the problem are of at least exponential time complexity. Problems for which there exist algorithms of *polynomial time complexity* (e.g. $O(n^k)$) are said to be *tractable*—that is, 'practically feasible'.

The branch of computer science that deals with the in/tractability of computational problems is a formal, mathematical domain called the *theory of computational complexity*, founded in the 1960s and early 1970s predominantly by the Israeli Michael Rabin, the Canadian Stephen Cook, and the Americans Juris Hartmanis, Richard Stearns, and Richard Karp.

Complexity theorists distinguish between two *problem classes* called **P** and **NP**, respectively. The formal (that is, mathematical) definitions of these classes are formidable, related to automata theory and, in particular, certain kinds of Turing machines (see Chapter 2), and they need not detain us here. Informally, the class **P** consists of all problems solvable in polynomial time—and these are, thus tractable. Informally, the class **NP** consists of problems for which a proposed solution, which may or may not be obtained in polynomial time, can be *checked* to be true in polynomial time. For example, the travelling salesman problem does not have a (known) polynomial time algorithmic solution but *given* a solution it can be 'easily' checked in polynomial time whether the solution is correct.

But, as noted, the travelling salesman problem is intractable. Thus, the **NP** class may contain problems believed to be intractable—although **NP** also contains the **P** class of tractable problems.

The implications of these ideas are considerable. Of particular interest is a concept called **NP**-completeness. A problem π is said to be *NP-complete* if π is in **NP** and all other problems in **NP** can be *transformed* or *reduced* in polynomial time to π. This means that if π is intractable then all other problems in **NP** are intractable. Conversely, if π is tractable, then all other problems in **NP** are also tractable. Thus, all the problems in **NP** are 'equivalent' in this sense.

In 1971, Stephen Cook introduced the concept of **NP**-completeness and proved that a particular problem called the 'satisfiability problem' is **NP**-complete. (The satisfiability problem involves

Boolean (or logical) expressions—for example the expression (a or b) and c, where the terms a, b, and c are Boolean (logical) variables having only the possible (truth) values TRUE and FALSE. The problems asks: 'Is there a set of truth values for the terms of a Boolean expression such that the value of the expression is TRUE?') Cook proved that any problem in **NP** can be reduced to the satisfiability problem which is also in **NP**. Thus, if the satisfiability problem is in/tractable then so is every other problem in **NP**.

This then raised the following question: *Are there polynomial time algorithms for all **NP** problems?* We noted earlier that **NP** contains **P**. But what this question asks is: Is **P** *identical to* **NP**? This is the so-called **P** = **NP** *problem*, arguably the most celebrated open problem in theoretical computer science. No one has proved that **P** = **NP**, and it is widely believed that this is not the case; that is, it is widely believed (but not yet proved) that **P** ≠ **NP**. This would mean that there are problems in **NP** (such as the travelling salesman and the satisfiability problems) that are not in **P**, hence are inherently intractable; and if they are **NP**-complete then all other problems reducible to them are also intractable. There are no practically feasible algorithms for such problems.

What the theory of **NP**-completeness tells us is that many seemingly distinct problems are *connected* in a strange sort of way. One can be transformed into another; they are equivalent to one another. We grasp the significance of this idea once we realize that a huge range of computational problems applicable in business, management, industry, and technology—'real world' problems—are **NP**-complete: if only one could construct a feasible (polynomial time) algorithm for one of these problems, one could find a feasible algorithm for all the others.

So how *does* one cope with such intractable problems? One common approach is the subject of Chapter 6.

Chapter 4
The art, science, and engineering of programming

To repeat, algorithmic thinking is central to computer science. Yet, algorithms are abstract artefacts. Computer scientists can live quite contentedly (if they so desired) in the rarified world of algorithms and never venture into the 'real world', much as 'pure' mathematicians might do. But if we desire real, physical computers to carry out computations on our behalf, if we want physical computers to not only do the kinds of computations we find too tedious (though necessary) but also those that are beyond our normal cognitive capacities, then algorithmic thinking alone does not suffice. They must be *implemented* in a form that can be communicated to physical computers, interpreted, and executed by them on their own terms rather than on human terms.

This is where programming enters the computing scene. A computer program is the specification of a desired computation in a language communicable to physical computers. The act of constructing such computations is called programming and the languages for specifying programs are called programming languages.

Programs are liminal artefacts

The concept of a program is elusive, subtle, and rather strange. For one thing, as I explain shortly, the same computation can be described at several abstraction levels depending on the language in which it is expressed, thus allowing for multiple *equivalent* programs. Secondly, a program is Janus-faced: on the one hand the program is a piece of static *text*, that is, a symbol structure that has all the characteristics of an abstract artefact. On the other hand, a program is a dynamic *process*—that is, it causes things to happen within a physical computer, and such processes consume physical time and physical space; thus it has a material substrate *upon* which it acts. Moreover, it requires a material medium *for* it to work.

Thus programs have an abstract and a material face, and for this, we may call programs *liminal* artefacts. The consequences of this liminality are both huge and controversial.

First, within the computer science community, some are drawn to the abstractness of programs and they hold the view that programs are *mathematical* objects. To them, programming is a kind of mathematical activity involving axioms, definitions, theorems, and proofs. Other computer scientists insist on its material facet and hold that programs are *empirical* objects. Programming to them is an empirical engineering activity involving the classical engineering tasks of specification of requirements, design, implementation, and conducting experiments that test and evaluate the resulting artefacts.

Secondly, the analogy between programs and the mind is often drawn. If a program is a liminal artificial object, the mind is a liminal natural object. On the one hand, mental (or cognitive) processes such as remembering, thinking, perceiving, planning, language understanding and mastering, etc., can be (and have been for centuries) examined as if the mind is a purely abstract thing interacting autonomously with the 'real' world. Yet the mind has a 'seat'. Unless one is an unrepentant dualist who completely separates mind from body, one does not believe that the mind can exist outside the brain—a physical object. And so, while some philosophers and cognitive scientists study the mind *as if* it is an abstract entity, neuroscientists seek strictly physical explanations of mental phenomena in terms of brain processes.

Indeed, the scientific study of cognition has been profoundly influenced by the analogy of mind with programs. One consequence has been the development of the branch of computer science called *artificial intelligence* (AI) which attempts to create mind-like and brain-like computational artefacts. Another has been the transformation of cognitive psychology into a broader discipline called *cognitive science* at the core of which is the hypothesis that mental processes can be modelled as program-like computations.

Thus, the intellectual influence of computer science has extended well beyond the discipline itself. Much as the Darwinian theory of evolution has extended its reach beyond biology so also because of the mind–program analogy computer science's influence has gone beyond computing itself. Or rather (as we will see in a later chapter) the very *idea* of computing has extended well beyond the scope of physical computers and automatic computation. I think it is fair to say that few sciences of the artificial have had such intellectual consequences outside their own domains.

Yet another consequence of the liminality of programs is that programs and programming are inexorably entwined with *artificial languages* called programming languages. One can design algorithms using natural language perhaps augmented with some artificial notation (as is seen in the case of the algorithms presented in Chapter 3). But no one can become a programmer without mastering at least one programming language. A pithy (if only rough) formula could well be:

Algorithms + Programming Languages = Programs

This itself has several implications.

One is the development of the theory of programming languages as a branch of computer science. Inevitably, this has led to a relationship between this theory and the science of linguistics, which is concerned with the structure of natural languages.

A second implication is the never-ending quest for the 'dream' programming language which can do what is required of any language better than any of its predecessors or its contemporary competitors. This is the activity of language design. The challenge to language designers is twofold: to facilitate communication of computations to physical computers which could then execute these computations with minimal human intervention; and also to facilitate communication with *other* human beings so that they can comprehend the computation, analyse it, criticize it, and offer suggestions for improvement, just as people do with any text. This dual challenge has been the source of an abiding obsession of computer scientists with programming and other languages of computation.

Closely related to language design is a third outcome: the study and development of programs called compilers that translate programs written in a programming language into the machine code of particular physical computers. Compiler design and implementation is yet another branch of computer science.

Finally, there has been the effort to design features of physical computers that facilitate the compiler's task. This activity is called 'language-oriented computer design' and has historically been of great interest within the branch of computer science called computer architecture (see Chapter 5).

Figure 3 shows schematically the many relationships of programs and programming with these other entities and disciplines. The entities enclosed in rectangles are contributing disciplines outside computer science; the entities enclosed in ovals are disciplines within computer science.

Legends

☐ Associated sciences

◇ Programs

◯ Disciplines in computer science associated with programming

3. **Programming, related disciplines, and associated sciences.**

Language, thought, reality, and programming

Notice, I say 'language' in the preceding section, not 'notation'. Notation refers to symbols invented for *writing* about something. Thus, chemical or mathematical notation. Language goes beyond notation in that it affords a symbol system for *thinking* about something. Language is embroiled with thought itself.

There is a famous issue which linguists and anthropologists have debated over: is thought *defined* by language? There are those who assert that this is so, that the language we use determines the way we think about the world and what we think about, indeed, that it *defines* our conceptualization of reality itself. Its most extreme implication is that since language is a defining element of culture, thoughts, percepts or concepts are not translatable from one language culture to another. We are each trapped in our own language-defined reality. A very post-modern condition. Others take the more moderate view that language *influences*, but does not define, how we think about the world. The proposition that language defines or influences thought is called the *Sapir–Whorf hypothesis* after the anthropological linguists Edward Sapir and Benjamin Lee Whorf who developed it. (It is also called the 'principle of linguistic relativity'.)

The Sapir–Whorf hypothesis addressed natural languages. Our concern is with artificial languages, specifically those invented to express computations. No one to my knowledge has framed an analogue to the Sapir–Whorf hypothesis for the computational realm but the obsession computer scientists have shown from the earliest days of electronic computers with programming and other computational languages strongly suggest that some form of the hypothesis is tacitly accepted by the computer science community. More accurately, we may say with some confidence that the languages of computing (in particular, programming) are intimately entwined with the nature of the computing environment; and that programming languages influence programmers' mentality.

So let us consider, first, programming languages. The nature of programs will naturally emerge from this discussion.

Programming languages as abstract artefacts

It was mentioned earlier that a computation can be specified as programs at different abstraction levels that vary in 'distance' from the physical computers that can execute the programs. Correspondingly, programming languages can be conceived at different abstraction levels. A crude dichotomy separates *high-level* from *low-level* languages. The former enable programs to be written independent of all physical computers that would execute them, and the latter refers to languages designed with respect to specific families of computers or even more specifically to a particular computer.

Thus, high-level languages are 'machine-independent' and low-level ones are 'machine-dependent' with the caveat that the degree of independence or dependence may well vary. The lowest level languages are called *assembly languages* and they are so specific to particular (family of, or individual) physical computers that the assembly language programmer literally manipulates the features of the computers themselves.

There was a time in the history of computing when almost all programming was done using assembly languages. Such programs were still symbol structures (and to a very moderate extent abstract) but translators called 'assemblers' (themselves programs) would convert them into the target computers' machine code. However, because of the tedium, difficulty, amount of human time required, and error-proneness of assembly language programming the focus shifted to the invention and design of increasingly higher level, machine-independent programming languages, and the task of translating programs in such languages into executable machine code for specific computers was delegated to compilers.

In this chapter hereafter, and in the remainder of this book, unless stated explicitly, the term 'programming language' will always refer to high-level languages.

Programming languages, in contrast to natural ones, are invented or designed. They are, thus, artefacts. They entail the use of notation as symbols. As we will see, a programming language is actually a set of symbol structures and, being independent of physical computers, are abstract in exactly the same sense that algorithms are abstract. We thus have the curious situation that while programs written in such languages are liminal, the languages of programming themselves are abstract.

Language = notation + concepts & categories

Let us revisit the notation/language distinction. The world of computing is populated by hundreds of computational languages. A large majority of these are for programming but others have been created for other purposes, in particular for the design and description of physical computers at various levels of abstraction (see Chapter 5). The latter are generically called 'computer hardware description languages' (CHDLs) or 'computer design and description languages' (CDDLs).

These computational languages employ different notations—symbols—and a part of the mental effort in learning a new computational language goes into mastering the notation—that is, what the symbols symbolize. This entails mapping the notational signs onto fundamental computational *concepts* and linguistic *categories*. A particular language, then, comprises a body of concepts and categories together with the notation that represents them. Again, as a rough formula:

$$\text{Concepts / Categories} + \text{Notation} = \text{Language}$$

In computing, different signs have been deployed in different languages to symbolize the same concept. Conversely, the same sign may symbolize different concepts in different languages.

For example, the fundamental programming concept known as the *assignment* (already encountered in Chapter 3) may be denoted by such signs as '=>', '=', '←', ':=' in different languages. Thus the assignment statements:

```
X + 1 => X
X = X + 1
X := X + 1
X ← X + 1
X += 1
```

Computer Science

all mean the same thing: the current value of the variable X is incremented by 1 and the result is assigned to (or copied back into) X. Assignment is a computational concept, and the assignment statement is a linguistic category, and is present in most programming languages. The ways of representing it differ from one language to another depending on the taste and predilection of the language designers.

Concepts and categories in programming languages

So what *are* these concepts and categories? Computing, recall, is symbol processing; in more common parlance it is information processing. 'In the beginning is information'—or, as language designers prefer to call it, data—which is to be processed. Thus a fundamental concept embedded in all programming languages is what is called the data type. As stated in Chapter 1, a data type defines the nature of the values a data object (otherwise called 'a variable') can hold along with the operations that are permissible ('legal') on such values. Data types are either 'primitive' (or 'atomic') or 'structured' (or 'composite'), composed from more basic data types.

In the factorial example of Chapter 3, there is only the primitive data type 'non-negative integer', meaning that integers greater than or equal to 0 are admissible as values of variables of this type; and only integer arithmetic operations can be performed on variables of this type. It also means that only integer values can be assigned to variables of this type. For example, an assignment such as

$$x \leftarrow x + 1$$

is a legal statement if x is defined as of data type integer. If x has not been declared as such, if instead it is declared as (say) a character string (representing a name), then the assignment will be illegal.

A number itself, is not necessarily an integer unless it is defined as such. Thus, from a computational point of view, a telephone number is not an integer; it is a numeric character string; one cannot add or multiply two telephone numbers. So, if x is declared as a numeric character string, the earlier assignment will not be valid.

The linear search algorithm of Chapter 3 includes both primitive and structured data types. The variable i is of the primitive type integer; the variable *given* is of structured type 'character string', itself composed out of the primitive type 'character'. The list *student* is also a structured data type, sometimes called 'linear list', sometimes 'array'. The i-th element of *student* is itself a structured data type (called by different names in different programming languages, including 'record' and 'tuple') comprising here of two data types, one (*name*) of type character string, the other (*email*) also of type character string. So a variable such as *student* is a hierarchically organized *data structure*: characters composed into character strings; character strings composed into tuples or records; tuples composed into lists or arrays.

But data or information is only the beginning of a computation. Moreover the variables themselves are passive. Computation involves action and the composition of actions into processes. A programming language, thus, must not only have the facility for specifying data objects, they must also include *statements* that specify actions and processes.

In fact, we have already encountered several times the most fundamental statement *types* in the preceding chapter. One is the assignment statement: its execution invokes a process that involves both a direction and a temporal flow of information. For example, in executing the assignment statement

$$A \leftarrow B$$

where A and B are both variables, information flows from B to A. But it isn't like water flowing from one container to another. The value of B is not changed or reduced or emptied after the execution of this statement. Rather, the value of B is 'read' and 'copied' into A so that at the end, the values of A and B are equal. However, in executing the statement

$$A \leftarrow A + B$$

the value of A does change: new value of A = old value of A + value of B. The value of B remains unchanged.

The general form of the assignment statement is

$$X \leftarrow E$$

where E is an *expression* (such as the arithmetic expressions $Y + 1$, $(X - Y) * (Z/W)$). The execution of the assignment in general is a two-step process: E is first evaluated; then this value is assigned to X.

The assignment statement, then, specifies the unit of action in a computation. It is the atomic process of computations. But just as in the natural world atoms combine into molecules and molecules into larger molecules so also in the computational world. Assignments combine to form larger segments, and the latter combine to form still larger segments until complete programs obtain. There is hierarchy at work in the computational world as there is in nature.

Thus, a major task of computer scientists has been to discover the *rules of composition*, invent statement types that represent these rules, and design notations for each statement type. While the rules of composition and statement types may be quite universal, different programming languages may use different notations to represent them.

One such statement type is the *sequential* statement: two or more (simpler) statements are composed sequentially so that when executed they are executed in the order of the component statements. The notation I used in Chapter 3 to denote sequencing was the ';'. Thus, in Euclid's algorithm we find the sequential statement

$m \leftarrow n;$
$n \leftarrow r;$
goto step 1

in which the flow of control proceeds through the three statements according to the order shown.

But computations may also require making choices between one of several alternatives. The **if . . . then . . . else** statements used in Chapter 3 in several of the algorithms are instances of the *conditional* statement type in programming languages. In the general form **if** C **then** $S1$ **else** $S2$, the condition C is evaluated, and if true then control goes to $S1$, otherwise control flows to $S2$.

Sometimes, we need to return flow of control to an earlier part of the computation and repeat it. The notations **while...do** and **repeat...until** used in the linear search and nonrecursive factorial algorithms in Chapter 3 exemplify these instances of the *iteration* statement type.

These three statement types, the sequential, conditional, and iterative, are the building blocks for the construction of programs. Every programming language provides notation to represent these categories. In fact, in principle, any computation can be specified by a program involving a combination of just these three statement types. (This was proved in 1966 by two Italian computer theorists, Corrado Böhm and Giuseppe Jacopini.) In practice many other rules of composition and corresponding statement types have been proposed to facilitate programming (such as the *unconditional branch* exemplified by the **goto** statement used in Euclid's algorithm in Chapter 3).

Programming as art

Programming is an act of design and like all design activities, it entails judgement, intuition, aesthetic taste, and experience. It is for this that Donald Knuth entitled his celebrated and influential series of texts *The Art of Computer Programming* (1968–9). Almost a decade later Knuth elaborated on this theme in a lecture. In speaking of the art of programming, he wrote, he was alluding to programming as an *art form*. Programs should be aesthetically satisfying; they should be beautiful. The experience of writing a program should be akin to composing poetry or music. Thus, the idea of *style*, so intimately a part of the discourses of art, music, and literature, must be an element of programming aesthetics.

Recall the Dutch computer scientist Edsger Dijkstra's remark mentioned in Chapter 3: in devising algorithms, 'Beauty is our business'. The Russian computer scientist A.P. Ershov has echoed these sentiments.

Along this same theme, Knuth later proposed that programs should be *works of literature*, that one can gain pleasure in writing programs in such a way that the programs will give pleasure on being read by others. (He called this philosophy 'literate programming', though I think 'literary programming' would have been more apt as an expression of his sentiment.)

Programming as a mathematical science

But, of course, computer scientists (including Knuth) seek to discover more objective and formal foundations for programming. They want a science of programming. The Böhm–Jacopini result mentioned earlier is the sort of formal, mathematical result computer scientists yearn for. In fact, by a 'science' of programming many computer scientists mean a *mathematical* science.

The view of programming as a mathematical science has been most prominently manifested in three other ways—all having to do with the abstract face of programs or, as I noted early in this chapter, the view held by some that programs are mathematical objects.

One is the discovery of *rules of syntax* of programming languages. These are rules that determine the grammatical correctness of programs and have a huge practical bearing, since one of the first tasks of compilers (automatic translators of high level programs into machine code) is to ensure that the program it is translating is grammatically or syntactically correct. The theory of programming language syntax owes its beginnings to the linguist Noam Chomsky's work on the theory of syntax (for natural languages).

The second contribution to the science of programming is the development of *rules of semantics*—that is, principles that define the meaning of the different statement types. Its importance should be quite evident: in order to use a programming language the programmer must be quite clear about the meaning of its component statement types. So also, the compiler writer must understand unambiguously the meaning of each statement type in order to translate programs into machine code. But semantics, as the term is used in linguistics, is a thorny problem since it involves relating linguistic categories to what they refer to in the world, and the theory of programming language semantics mirrors these same difficulties. It is fair to say that the theory of semantics in programming, despite its sophisticated development, has not had the same kind of acceptance by the computer science community, nor has it been used so effectively as the theory of syntax.

The third contribution to the science of programming is closely related to the semantics issue. This contribution is founded on the conviction of such computer scientists as the Englishman C.A.R. Hoare and the Dutchman Edsger Dijkstra that computing is akin to mathematics and that the same principles that mathematicians use, such as axioms, rules of deductive logic, theorems, and proofs, are applicable to programming. This philosophy was stated quite unequivocally and defiantly by Hoare who announced, in 1985, the following manifesto:

(a) *Computers are mathematical machines*. That is, their behaviour can be mathematically defined and every detail is logically derivable from the definition.

(b) *Programs are mathematical expressions*. They describe precisely and in detail the behaviour of the computer on which they are executed.

(c) *A programming language is a mathematical theory*. It is a formal system which helps the programmer in both developing a program and proving that the program satisfies the specification of its requirements.

(d) *Programming is a mathematical activity*. Its practice requires application of the traditional methods of mathematical understanding and proof.

In the venerable axiomatic tradition in mathematics, one begins with axioms (propositions that are taken to be 'self-evidently' true about the domain of interest, such as the principle of mathematical induction mentioned in Chapter 3), and definitions of basic concepts, and *proves* progressively, new insights and propositions (collectively called theorems) from these axioms, definitions and already proved theorems, using rules of deduction. Inspired by this tradition, the third contribution to a mathematical science of programming concerns the construction of axiomatic proofs of the correctness of programs based on axioms, definitions and rules of deduction defining the semantics of the relevant programming language. The semantics is called *axiomatic semantics*, and their application is known as axiomatic proofs of correctness.

As in the axiomatic approach in mathematics (and its use in such disciplines as mathematical physics and economics), there is much formal elegance and beauty in the mathematical science of programming. However, it is only fair to point out that while a formidable body of knowledge has been developed in this realm, a goodly number of academic computer scientists and industrial practitioners remain skeptical of their practical applicability in the hurly-burly 'real world' of computing.

Programming as (software) engineering

This is because of the view held by many that programs are not 'just' beautiful abstract artefacts. Even Hoare's manifesto recognized that programs must describe the behaviour of the *computers* which execute them. The latter is the material face of programs and which confers liminality to them. To many, in fact, programs are technological products, hence programming is an engineering activity.

The word *software* appears to have entered the computing vocabulary in 1960. Yet its connotation remains uncertain. Some use 'software' and 'program' as synonyms. Some think of software to mean the special and essential set of programs (such as operating systems and other tools and 'utilities' called, collectively, 'system programs') that are built to execute atop a physical computer to create the virtual machines (or computer systems) that others can use more efficaciously (see Figure 1 in Chapter 2). Still others consider software to mean not only programs but the associated documentation that is essential to the development, operation, maintenance and modification of large programs. And there are some who would include human expertise and knowledge in this compendium.

At any rate, 'software' has the following significant connotations: it is that part of a computer system that is not itself physical; it requires the physical computer to make it operational; and there is a sense in which software is very much an *industrial* product with all that the adjective implies.

Software is, then, a computational artefact that facilitates the usage of a computer system by many (possibly millions, even billions of) users. Most times (though not always) it is a commercially produced artefact which manifests certain levels of robustness and reliability we have come to expect of industrial systems.

Perhaps in analogy with other industrial systems, a software development project is associated with a *life cycle*. And so, like many other complex, engineering projects (e.g. a new space satellite launch project) the development of a software system is regarded as an engineering project, and it is in this context that the term *software engineering* (first coined in the mid-1960s) seems particularly apposite. This has led, naturally, to the idea of the 'software engineer'. It is not a coincidence that a large portion of thinking about software engineering has originated in the industrial sector.

Various models of the software life cycle have been proposed over the past fifty years. Collectively, they all recognize that the development of a software system involves a number of stages:

(a) Analysis of the requirements the software is intended to serve.

(b) Development of precise functional, performance and cost specifications of the different components ('modules') that can be identified from requirements analysis.

(c) The design of the software system that will (hopefully) meet the specifications. This activity may itself consist of conceptual and detailed design stages.

(d) Implementing the design as an operational software system specified in a programming language and compiled for execution on the target computer system(s).

(e) Verification and validation of the implemented set of programs to ensure that they meet the specifications.

(f) Once verified and validated, the maintenance of the system and, if and whenever necessary, its modification.

These stages do not, of course, follow in a rigidly linear way. There is always the possibility of returning to an earlier stage from a later one if flaws and faults are discovered. Moreover, this software life cycle also requires an infrastructure—of tools, methodology, documentation standards, and human expertise which collectively constitute a software engineering *environment*.

One must also note that one or more of these stages will entail solid bodies of scientific theories as part of their deployment. Specification and design may involve the use of languages having their own syntax and semantics; detailed design and implementation will involve programming languages and, possibly, the use of axiomatic proof techniques. Verification and validation will invariably demand sophisticated modes of proving and experimentally testing the software. Much as the classical fields of engineering (such as structural or mechanical engineering) entail engineering sciences as components, so also software engineering.

Chapter 5
The discipline of computer architecture

The physical computer is at the bottom of the hierarchy MY_COMPUTER shown in Figure 1. In everyday parlance the physical computer is referred to as *hardware*. It is 'hard' in that it is a physical artefact that ultimately obeys the laws of nature. The physical computer is the fundamental *material* computational artefact of interest to computer scientists.

But if someone asks: 'What is the nature of the physical computer?' I may equivocate in my answer. This is because the physical computer, though a part of a larger hierarchy, is itself complex enough that it manifests its own internal hierarchy. Thus it can be designed and described at multiple levels of abstraction. The relationship between these levels combine the principles of compositional, abstraction/refinement, and constructive hierarchy discussed in Chapter 1.

Perhaps the most significant aspect of this hierarchy from a computer scientist's perspective (and we owe it, in major part, to the genius of the Hungarian-American mathematician and scientific gadfly John von Neumann to first recognize it) is the distinction of the physical computer as a symbol processing computational artefact from the physical components, obeying the laws of physics, that realize this artefact. This separation is important. As a symbol processor, the computer is abstract in exactly the same sense that software is abstract; yet, like software this abstract artefact has no existence without its physical implementation.

The view of the physical computer as an abstract, symbol processing computational artefact constitutes the computer's *architecture*. (I have used the term 'architecture' before to mean the functional structure of the virtual machines shown in Figure 1. But now, 'computer architecture' has a more specific technical connotation.) The physical (digital) components that implement the architecture—the actual hardware—constitutes its *technology*. We thus have this distinction between 'computer architecture' and (digital) technology.

There is another important aspect of this distinction. A given architecture can be implemented using different technologies. Architectures are not independent of technologies in that developments in the latter influence architecture design, but there is a certain amount of autonomy or 'degrees of freedom' the designer of computer architectures enjoy. Conversely, the design of an architecture might shape the kind of technology deployed.

To draw an analogy, consider an institution such as a university. This has both its abstract and material characteristics. The organization of the university, its various administrative and academic units, their internal structure and functions, and so on, is the analogue to a computer's architecture. One can design a university (it is, after all, an artefact), describe it, discuss and analyse it, criticize it, alter its structure, just as one can any other abstract entity. But a university is implemented by way of human and physical resources. They are the analogue to a computer's (hardware) technology. Thus, while the design or evolution of a university entails a considerable degree of autonomy, its realization can only depend on the nature, availability and efficacy of its resources (the people employed, the buildings, the equipment, the physical space, the campus structure as a whole, etc.). Conversely, the design of a university's organization will influence the kinds of resources that have to be in place.

So here are the key terms for this discussion: *computer architecture* is the discipline within computer science concerned with the design, description, analysis, and study of the logical organization, behaviour, and functional elements of a physical computer; all of that constitutes the (physical) computer's architecture. The task of the computer *architect* is to design architectures that satisfy the needs of the users of the physical computer (software engineers, programmers and algorithm designers, non-technical users) on the one hand and yet are economically and technologically viable.

Computer architectures are thus liminal artefacts. The computer architect must navigate delicately between the Scylla of the computer's functional and performance requirements and the Charybdis of technological feasibility.

Solipsistic and sociable computers

The globalization of everything owes much to the computer. If 'no man is an island entire of itself', then nor in the 21st century is the computer. But once upon a time, and for many years, computers did indeed exist as islands of their own. A computational artefact of the kind depicted as TEXT in Figure 1 would go about its tasks as if the world beyond did not exist. Its only interaction with the environment was by way of input data and commands and its output results. Other than that, for all practical purposes, the physical computer, along with its dedicated system and application programs and other tools (such as programming languages), lived in splendid, solipsistic isolation.

But, as just noted, few computers are solipsistic nowadays. The advent of the Internet, the institution of emails, the World Wide Web, and the various forms of social media have put paid to computational solipsism. Even the most reclusive user's laptop or smart phone is a sociable computer as soon as that user goes online to purchase a book or check out the weather or seek directions to go to some place. His computer is sociable in that it interacts and communicates with innumerable other computers (though blissfully unknown to him) physically located all over the planet through the network that is the Internet. Indeed, every emailer, every seeker of information, every watcher of an online video is not just using the Internet: her computer is part *of* the Internet. Or rather, the Internet is one global interactive community of sociable computational artefacts and human agents.

But there are more modest networks of which a computer can be a part. Machines within an organization (such as a university or a company) are connected to one another through what are called 'local area networks'. And a constellation of computers distributed over a region may collaborate, each performing its own computational task but exchanging information as and when needed. Such systems are traditionally called *multicomputing* or *distributed computing* systems.

The management of multicomputing or distributed computing or Internet computing is effected by a combination of network principles called 'protocols' and extremely sophisticated software systems. When we consider the discipline of computer architecture, however, it is the individual computer, whether solipsistic or sociable, that commands our attention. It is this I discuss in the remainder of this chapter.

Outer and inner architectures

The word 'architecture' in the context of computers was first used in the early 1960s by three IBM engineers, Gene Amdahl, Frederick Brooks, and Gerrit Blaauw. They used this term to mean the collection of functional attributes of a physical computer as available to the lowest level programmer of the computer (system programmers who build operating systems, compilers, and other basic utilities using assembly languages); its 'outer façade' so to speak. Since then, however, the practice of computer architecture has extended to include the internal logical, structural, and functional organization and behaviour of the physical (hardware) components of the machine. Thus, in practice, 'computer architecture' refers to the functional and logical aspects of both the outer façade and the interior of a physical computer. Yet, no agreed upon terms exist for these two aspects; here, for simplicity, I will call them 'outer' and 'inner' architectures, respectively.

The two are hierarchically related. They are two different abstractions of the physical computer, with the outer architecture an abstraction of the inner one or, conversely, the inner architecture a refinement of the outer one. Or, depending on the design strategy used, one may regard a computer's inner architecture as an implementation of the outer one.

The design of outer computer architectures is shaped by forces exerted from the computer's computational environment: since the outer architecture is the interface between the physical computer and system programmers who create the virtual machines the 'ordinary' users of the computer 'see', it is natural that the functional requirements demanded by this environment will exert an influence on the outer architectural design. For example, if the computer *C* is intended to support the efficient execution of programs written in a particular kind of language, say *L*, then the outer architecture of *C* may be oriented toward the features of *L*; thus easing the task of the language compiler in translating programs written in *L* into machine code for *C*. Or if the operating system *OS* that sits atop *C* has certain facilities, then the implementation of *OS* may be facilitated by appropriate features incorporated into *C*'s outer architecture.

On the other hand, since a computer's inner architecture will be implemented by physical (hardware) components, and these

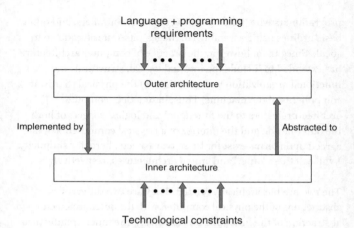

4. Computer architectures and their external constraints.

components are built using a particular kind of technology T, the design of the inner architecture will be constrained by features of T.

At the same time, the design of the outer architecture may be shaped and constrained by the nature of the inner architecture and vice versa. Thus, there is an intimate relationship between the computational environment, the outer architecture of the computer, its inner architecture, and the physical technology (Figure 4).

The outer architecture

The *sanctum sanctorum* of a computer's outer architecture is its *instruction set*, which specifies the repertoire of operations the computer can be directly commanded to perform by a programmer. Exactly what types of operations can be performed will both determine and be determined by the set of *data types* the computer directly supports or 'recognizes'. For example, if the computer is intended to efficiently support scientific and engineering computations the significant data types will be real numbers (e.g. 6.483, 4 * 10[8], − 0.000021, etc.) and integers. Thus the instruction set should include a range of arithmetic instructions.

In addition to such domain-specific instructions, there will always be a repertoire of general purpose instructions, for example, for implementing conditional (e.g. **if then else**), iterative (e.g. **while do**) and unconditional branch (e.g. **goto**) kinds of programming language constructs. Other instructions may enable a program to be organized into segments or modules responsible for different kinds of computations, with the capability of transferring control from one module to another.

An instruction is really a 'packet' that describes the operation to be performed along with references to the locations ('addresses') of its input data objects ('operands' in architectural vocabulary) and the location of where its output data will be placed. This idea of *address* implies a *memory* space. Thus, there are memory components as part of an outer architecture. Moreover, these components generally form a hierarchy:

LONG-TERM MEMORY—known as 'backing store', 'secondary memory', or 'hard drive'.

MEDIUM-TERM MEMORY—otherwise known as 'main memory'.

VERY SHORT-TERM (WORKING) MEMORY—known as registers.

This is a hierarchy in terms of retentivity of information, size capacity, and speed of access. Thus, even though an outer architecture is abstract, the material aspect of the physical computer is rendered visible: space (size capacity) and time are physical, measured in physical units (bits or bytes of information, nanoseconds or picoseconds of time, etc.) not abstract. It is this combination that makes a computer architecture (outer or inner) a liminal artefact.

The long-term memory is the longest in retentivity (in its capacity to 'remember')—permanent, for all practical purposes. It is also the largest in size capacity, but slowest in access speed. Medium-term memory retains information only as long as the computer is operational. The information is lost when the computer is powered off. Its size capacity is far less than that of long-term memory but its access time is far shorter than that of long-term memory. Short-term or working memory may change its contents many times in the course of a single computation; its size capacity is several orders of magnitude lower than that of medium-term memory, but its access time is much less than that of long-term memory.

The reason for a memory hierarchy is to maintain a judicious balance between retentivity, and space and time demands for computations. There will be also instructions in the instruction set to effect transfers of programs and data between these memory components.

The other features of outer architecture are built around the instruction set and its set of data types. For example, instructions must have ways of identifying the locations ('addresses') in memory of the operands and of instructions. The different ways of identifying memory addresses are called 'addressing modes'. There will also be rules or conventions for organizing and encoding instructions of various types so that they may be efficiently held in memory; such conventions are called 'instruction formats'. Likewise, 'data formats' are conventions for organizing various data types; data objects of a particular data type are held in memory according to the relevant data format.

Finally, an important architectural parameter is the *word length*. This determines the amount of information (measured in number of bits) that can be *simultaneously* read from or written into medium-term (main) memory. The speed of executing an instruction is very much dependent on word length, as also the range of data that can be accessed per unit time.

Here are a few typical examples of computer instructions (or *machine instructions*, a term I have already used before) written in symbolic (assembly language) notation, along with their semantics (that is the actions these instructions cause to happen).

Instruction	Meaning (Action)
1. LOAD R2, (R1, D)	R2 ← main-memory [R1 + D]
2. ADD R2, 1	R2 ← R2 + 1
3. JUMP R1, D	**goto** main-memory [R1 + D]

Legend:

R1, R2: registers

main-memory: medium-term memory

1: the integer constant '1'

D: an integer number

'R1 + D' in (1) adds the number 'D' to the *contents* of register R1 and this determines the main-memory address of an operand. 'R1 + D' in (3) computes an address likewise but this address is interpreted as that of an instruction in main-memory to which control is transferred.

The inner architecture

A physical computer is ultimately a complex of circuits, wires, and other physical components. In principle, the outer architecture can be explained as the outcome of the structure and behaviour of these physical components. However, the conceptual distance between an abstract artefact like an outer architecture and the physical circuits is so large that it is no more meaningful to attempt such an explanation than it is to explain or describe a whole living organism (except perhaps bacteria and viruses) in terms of its cell biology. Cell biology does not suffice to explain, say, the structure and functioning of the cardio-vascular system. Entities above the cell level (e.g. tissues and organs) need to be understood before the whole system can be understood. So also, digital circuit theory does not suffice to explain the outer architecture of a computer, be it a laptop or the world's most powerful supercomputer.

This conceptual distance in the case of computers—sometimes called 'semantic gap'—is bridged in a hierarchic fashion. The implementation of an outer architecture is explained in terms of the inner architecture and its components. If the inner architecture is itself complex and there is still a conceptual distance from the circuit level, then the inner architecture is described and explained in terms of a still lower level of abstraction called *microarchitecture*. The latter in turn may be refined to what is called the 'logic level', and this may be sufficiently close to the circuit level that it can be implemented in terms of the latter components. Broadly speaking, a physical computer will admit of the following levels of description/abstraction:

Level 4: Outer architecture
Level 3: Inner architecture
Level 2: Microarchitecture
Level 1: Logic level
Level 0: Circuit level

Computer architects *generally* concern themselves with the outer and inner architectures, and a refinement of the inner architecture which is shown earlier as microarchitecture (this refinement is explained later). They are interested not only in the features constituting these architectural levels but also the relationship between them.

The principal components of a computer's inner architecture are shown in Figure 5. It consists of the following. First, a *memory system* which includes the memory hierarchy visible in the outer architecture but includes other components that are only visible in the inner architectural level. This system includes controllers responsible for the management of information (symbol

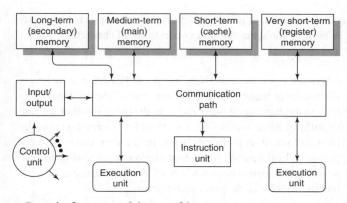

5. Portrait of a computer's inner architecture.

structures) that pass between the memories in the hierarchy, and between the system and the rest of the computer. Second, one or more *instruction interpretation units* which prepare instructions for execution and control their execution. Third, one or more *execution units* responsible for the actual execution of the various classes of instructions demanded in a computation. (Collectively, the instruction interpretation system(s) and execution unit(s) are called the computer's *processor*.) Fourth, a *communication network* that serve to transfer symbol structures between the other functional components. Fifth, an *input/output system* responsible for receiving symbol structures from, and sending symbol structures to, the physical computer's environment. And finally, the *control unit* which is responsible for issuing signals that control the activities of the other components.

The execution units are rather like the organs of a living body. They can be highly specialized for operations of specific sorts on specific data types, or more general purpose units capable of performing comprehensive sets of operations. For example, one execution unit may be dedicated to performing only integer arithmetic operations while another is specialized for arithmetic operations on real numbers; a third only manipulates bit strings in various ways; another does operations on character strings, and so on.

Internally, a processor will have its own dedicated, extremely short-term or *transient*, memory elements (of shorter term retentivity than the registers visible in the outer architecture, and sometimes called 'buffer registers') to which information must be brought from other memories before instructions can be actually processed by the instruction interpretation or processing units. Such buffer registers form the 'lowest' level in the memory hierarchy visible in the inner architecture.

There is yet another component of the memory hierarchy visible in the inner architecture but (usually) abstracted away in the outer architecture. This is a memory element called *cache* memory that lies between the medium-term (main) memory and the very short-term (register) memory. In Figure 5, this is shown as 'short-term memory'. Its capacity and speed of access lie between the two. The basic idea of a cache is that since instructions within a program module execute (usually) in sequence, a chunk of instructions can be placed in the cache so that instructions can be accessed more rapidly than if main memory is accessed. Likewise, the nature of program behaviour is such that data is also often accessed from sequential addresses in main memory so data chunks may also be placed in a cache. Only when the relevant instruction or data object is not found in the cache, will main memory be accessed, and this will cause a chunk of information in the cache to be replaced by the new chunk in which the relevant information is located so that future references to instructions and data will be available in the cache.

'The computer-within-the-computer'

So how can we connect the outer to the inner architecture? How do they actually relate? To understand this we need to understand the function of the *control unit* (which, in Figure 5 stands in splendid black box-like isolation).

The control unit is, metaphorically, the computer's brain, a kind of homunculus, and is sometimes described as a 'computer-within-the-computer'. It is the organ which manages, controls, and sequences all the activities of the other systems, and the movement of symbol structures between them. It does so by issuing *control signals* (symbol structures that are categorically distinct from instructions and data) to other parts of the machine as and when required. It is the puppeteer that pulls the strings to activate the other puppet-like systems.

In particular, the control unit issues signals to the processor (the combination of the instruction interpretation and execution units) to cause a repetitive algorithm usually called the *instruction cycle* (ICycle for short) to be executed by the processor. It is the ICycle which ties the outer to the inner architecture. The general form of this is as follows:

ICYCLE:
Input: *main-memory*: medium-term memory; *registers*: short-term memory;

Internal: *pc*: transient buffer; *ir*: transient buffer; *or*: transient buffer

{*pc*, short for 'program counter', holds the address of the next instruction to be executed; *ir*, 'instruction register', holds the current instruction to be executed; *or* will hold the values of the operands of an instruction}.

FETCH INSTRUCTION: Using value of pc transfer instruction from main-memory to *ir* ($ir \leftarrow$ main-memory [*pc*])

DECODE the operation part of instruction in *ir*;

CALCULATE OPERAND ADDRESSES: decode the address modes of operands in instruction in *ir* and determine the effective addresses of operands and result locations in main-memory or registers.

FETCH OPERANDS from memory system into *or*.

EXECUTE the operation specified in the instruction in *ir* using the operand values in *or* as inputs.

STORE result of the operation in the destination location for result specified in *ir*.

UPDATE PC: if the operation performed in EXECUTE is not a **goto** type operation then $pc \leftarrow pc + 1$. Otherwise do nothing: EXECUTE will have placed the address of the target **goto** instruction in *ir* into *pc*.

The ICycle is controlled by the control unit but it is the instruction interpretation unit that performs the FETCH INSTRUCTION through FETCH OPERANDS steps of the ICycle, and then the STORE and UPDATE steps, and an execution unit will perform the EXECUTE step. As a specific example consider the LOAD instruction described earlier:

LOAD R2, (R1, D)

Notice that the semantics of this instruction *at the outer architectural* level is simply

R2 $\leftarrow$ Main-memory [R1 + D]

At the *inner architectural* level, its execution entails the performance of the ICycle. The instruction is FETCHed into *ir*, it is DECODEd, the operand addresses are CALCULATEd, the operands are FETCHed, the instruction is EXECUTEd, and the result STOREd into register R2. All these steps of the ICycle are abstracted out in the outer architecture as unnecessary detail as far as the users of the outer architecture (the system programmers) are concerned.

Microprogramming

To repeat, the ICycle is an algorithm whose steps are under the control of the control unit. In fact, one might grasp easily that this algorithm can be implemented *as a program executed by the control unit* with the rest of the computer (the memory system, the instruction interpretation unit, the execution units, the communication pathways, the input/output system) as part of the 'program's' *environment*. This insight, and the design of the architecture of the control unit based on this insight, was named *microprogramming* by its inventor, British computer pioneer Maurice Wilkes. And it is in the sense that the microprogrammed control unit executes a microprogram that implements the ICycle for each distinct type of instruction that led some to call the microprogrammed control unit the computer-within-the-computer. In fact, the architecture of the computer as the *microprogrammer* sees it is necessarily more refined than the inner architecture indicated in Figure 5. This microprogrammer's (or control unit implementer's) view of the computer is the 'microarchitecture' mentioned earlier.

Parallel computing

It is in the nature of those who make artefacts ('artificers')— engineers, artists, craftspeople, writers, etc.—to be never satisfied with what they have made; they desire to constantly make better artefacts (whatever the criterion of 'betterness' is). In the realm of physical computers the two dominant desiderata are space and time: to make smaller and faster machines.

One strategy for achieving these goals is by way of improving physical technology. This is a matter of solid state physics, electronics, fabrication technology, and circuit design. The extraordinary progress over the sixty or so years since the integrated circuit was first created, producing increasingly denser and increasingly smaller components and the concentration of ever increasing computing power in such components is evident to all who use laptops, tablets, and smart phones. There is a celebrated conjecture—called Moore's law, after its inventor, American engineer Gordon Moore—that the density of basic circuit components on a single chip doubles approximately every two years, which has been empirically borne out over the years.

But *given* a particular state of the art of physical technology, computer architects have evolved techniques to increase the *throughput* or *speedup* of computations, measured, for example, by such metrics as the number of instructions processed per unit time or the number of some critical operations (such as real number arithmetic operations in the case of a computer dedicated to scientific or engineering computations) per unit time. These architectural strategies fall under the rubric of *parallel processing*.

The basic idea is quite straightforward. Two processes or tasks, *T1, T2* are said to be executable in parallel if they occur in a *sequential task stream* (such as instructions in a sequential program) and are mutually independent. This mutual independence is achieved if they satisfy some particular conditions. The exact nature and complexity of the conditions will depend on several factors, specifically:

(a) The nature of the tasks.

(b) The structure of the task stream, e.g. whether it contains iterations (**while do** types of tasks), conditionals (**if then else**s) or **goto**s.

(c) The nature of the units that execute the tasks.

Consider, for example, the situation in which two identical processors share a memory system. We want to know under what conditions two tasks T1, T2 appearing in a sequential task stream can be initiated in parallel.

Suppose the set of input data objects to and the set of output data objects from T1 are designated as INPUT1 and OUTPUT1 respectively. Likewise, for T2, we have INPUT2 and OUTPUT2 respectively. Assume that these inputs and outputs are locations in main memory and/or registers. Then T1 and T2 can be executed in parallel (symbolized as *T1 || T2*) if *all* the following conditions are satisfied:

(a) INPUT1 and OUTPUT2 are *independent*. (That is, they have nothing in common.)

(b) INPUT2 and OUTPUT1 are independent.

(c) OUTPUT1 and OUTPUT 2 are independent.

These are known as *Bernstein's conditions* after the computer scientist A.J. Bernstein, who first formalized them. If any one of the three conditions are not met, then there is a *data dependency* relation between them, and the tasks cannot be executed in parallel. Consider, as a simple example, a segment of a program stream consisting of the following assignment statements

[1] $A \leftarrow B + C$;
[2] $D \leftarrow B * F/E$;
[3] $X \leftarrow A - D$;
[4] $W \leftarrow B - F$.

Thus:

INPUT1 = {*B, C*}, OUTPUT1 = {*A*}
INPUT2 = {*B, E, F*}, OUTPUT2 = {*D*}
INPUT3 = {*A, D*}, OUTPUT3 = {*X*}
INPUT4 = {*B, F*}, OUTPUT4 = {*W*}

Applying Bernstein's condition, it can be seen that (i) statements [1] and [2] can be executed in parallel; (ii) statements [3] and [4] can be executed in parallel; however, (iii) statements [1] and [3] have a data dependency (variable *A*); (iv) statements [2] and [3] have a data dependency constraint (variable *D*); thus these pairs cannot be executed in parallel.

So, in effect, taking these parallel and non-parallel conditions into account, and assuming that there are enough processors that can execute parallel statements simultaneously, the actual ordering of execution of the statements would be:

    Statements [1] || Statement [2];
    Statement [3] || Statement [4].

This sequential/parallel ordering illustrates the structure of a *parallel program* in which the tasks are individual statements described using a programming language. But consider the physical computer itself. The goal of research in parallel processing is broadly twofold: (a) Inventing algorithms or strategies that can detect parallelism between tasks and schedule or assign parallel tasks to different task execution units in a computer system. (b) Designing computers that support parallel processing.

From a computer architect's perspective the potential for parallelism exists at several levels of abstraction. Some of these *levels of parallelism* are:

(1) Task (or instruction) streams executing concurrently on independent data streams, on distinct, multiple processors but with the task streams communicating with one another (for example, by passing messages to one another or transmitting data to one another).

(2) Task (or instruction) streams executing concurrently on a single shared data stream, on multiple processors within a single computer.

(3) Multiple data streams occupying multiple memory units, accessed concurrently by a single task (instruction) stream executing on a single processor.

(4) Segments (called 'threads') of a single task stream, executing concurrently on either a single processor or multiple processors.

(5) The stages or steps of a single instruction executing concurrently within the ICycle.

(6) Parts of a microprogram executed concurrently within a computer's control unit.

All parallel processing architectures exploit variations of the possibilities just discussed, often in combination.

Consider, as an example, the abstraction level (5) given earlier. Here, the idea is that since the ICycle consists of several stages (from FETCH INSTRUCTION to UPDATE pc), the processor itself that executes the ICycle can be organized in the form of a *pipeline* consisting of these many stages. A single instruction will go through all the stages of the pipeline in sequential fashion. The 'tasks' at this level of abstraction are the steps of the ICycle through which an instruction moves. However, when an instruction occupies one of the stages, the other stages are free and they can be processing the relevant stages of other instructions in the instruction stream. Ideally, a seven-step ICycle can be executed by a seven-stage instruction processor pipeline, and all the stages of the pipeline are busy, working on seven different instructions in parallel, in an assembly line fashion. This, of course, is the ideal condition. In practice, Bernstein's conditions may be violated by instruction pairs in the instruction stream and so the pipeline may have stages that are 'empty' because of data dependency constraints between stages of instruction pairs.

Architectures that support this type of parallel processing are called *pipelined* architectures (Figure 6).

As another example, consider tasks at abstraction level (1) presented earlier. Here, multiple processors (also called 'cores')—within

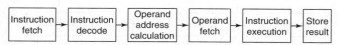

6. An instruction pipeline.

the same computer—execute instruction streams (belonging to, say, distinct program modules) in parallel. These processors may be accessing a single shared memory system or the memory system itself may be decomposed into distinct memory modules. At any rate, a sophisticated 'processor-memory interconnection network' (or 'switch') will serve as the interface between the memory systems and the processors (Figure 7). Such schemes are called *multiprocessor* architectures.

As mentioned before, the objective of parallel processing architectures is to increase the *throughput* or *speedup* of a computer system through purely architectural means. However, as the small example of the four assignment statements illustrated, there are limits to the 'parallelization' of a task stream because of data dependency constraints; thus, there are limits to the speedup that can be attained in a parallel processing environment. This limit was quantitatively formulated in the 1960s by computer designer Gene Amdahl, who stated that the potential speedup of a parallel processing computer is limited by that part of the computation that cannot be parallelized. Thus the speedup effect of increasing the number of parallel execution units levels off after a certain point. This principle is called *Amdahl's law*.

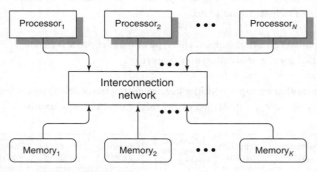

7. **Portrait of a multiprocessor.**

The science in computer architecture

The reader having reached this section of the chapter may well ask: granted that computer architectures are liminal artefacts, in what sense is the discipline a science of the artificial?

To answer this question we must recognize that the most striking aspect of the discipline is that its knowledge space consists (mainly) of a body of *heuristic* principles, and the kind of reasoning used in designing computer architectures is *heuristic reasoning*.

Heuristics—from the Greek word *hurisko*, 'to find'—are rules or propositions that offer hope or promise of solutions to certain kinds of problems (discussed in the next chapter) but *there is no guarantee of success*. To paraphrase Hungarian-American mathematician George Polya who famously recognized the role of heuristics in mathematical discovery, heuristic thinking is never definite, never final, never *certain*; rather, it is provisional, plausible, tentative.

We are often obliged to use heuristics because we may not have any other option. Heuristics are invoked in the absence of more formal, more certain, theory-based principles. The divide-and-conquer principle discussed in Chapter 3 is an example of an ubiquitous heuristic used in problem solving and decision making. It is a plausible principle which might be expected to help solve a complex problem but is not guaranteed to succeed in a particular case. Experiential knowledge is the source of many heuristics. The rule 'if it is cloudy, take an umbrella' is an example. The umbrella may well be justified but not always.

The use of heuristics brings with it the necessity of *experiment*. Since heuristics are not assured of success the only recourse is to apply them to a particular problem and see empirically if it works;

that is, conduct an experiment. Conversely, heuristic principles may themselves be derived based on prior experiments. *Heuristics and experiments go hand in hand*, an insight such pioneers in heuristic thinking as Allen Newell and Herbert Simon, and pioneers of computer design such as Maurice Wilkes fully grasped.

All this is a prelude to the following: *The discipline of computer architecture is an experimental, heuristic science of the artificial.*

Over the decades since the advent of the electronic digital computer, a body of rules, principles, precepts, propositions, and schemas have come into being concerning the design of computer architectures, almost all of which are heuristic in nature. The idea of a memory hierarchy as a design principle is an example. The principle of pipelining is another. They arise from experiential knowledge, drawing analogies, and common sense observations.

For example, experiences with prior architecture design and the difficulties faced in producing machine code using compilers have yielded heuristic principles to eliminate the difficulties. In the 1980s, the computer scientist William Wulf proposed several such heuristics based on experience with the design of compilers for certain computers. Here are some of them:

> *Regularity.* If a particular (architectural) feature is realized in a certain way in one part of the architecture then it should be realized in the same way in all parts.

> *Separation of concerns.* (Divide and rule.) The overall architecture should be partitionable into a number of independent features, each of which can be designed separately.

> *Composability.* By virtue of the two foregoing principles it should be possible to compose the separate independent features in arbitrary ways.

But experiments must follow the incorporation of heuristic principles into a design. Such experiments may entail implementing a 'prototype' or experimental machine and conducting tests on it. Or it may involve constructing a (software) simulation model of the architecture and conducting experiments on the simulated architecture.

In either case the experiments may reveal flaws in the design, in which case the outcome would be to modify the design by rejecting some principles and inserting others; and then repeat the cycle of experimentation, evaluation, and modification.

This schema is, of course, almost identical to the model of scientific problem solving advanced by philosopher of science Karl Popper:

$$P1 \rightarrow TT \rightarrow EE \rightarrow P2$$

Here, *P1* is the 'current' problem situation; *TT* is a tentative theory advanced to explain or solve the problem situation; *EE* is the process of error elimination applied to *TT* (by way of experiments and/or critical reasoning); and *P2* is the resulting new problem situation after the errors have been eliminated. In the context of computer architecture, *P1* is the design problem, specified in terms of goals and requirements the eventual computer must satisfy; *TT* is the heuristics-based design itself (which is a *theory of the computer*); *EE* is the process of experimentation and evaluation of the design, and the elimination of its flaws and limitations; and the *outcome P2* is a possibly modified set of goals and requirements constituting a new design problem.

Chapter 6
Heuristic computing

Many problems are not conducive to algorithmic solutions. A parent teaching her child to ride a bicycle cannot present to the child an algorithm he can learn and apply in the way he can learn how to multiply two numbers. A teacher of creative writing or of painting cannot offer students algorithms for writing magical realist fiction or painting abstract expressionist canvases.

This inability is in part because of one's ignorance (even that of a professor of creative writing) or lack of understanding of the exact nature of such tasks. The painter wants to capture the texture of a velvet gown, the solidity of an apple, the enigma of a smile. But what constitutes that velvetiness, that solidity, that enigmatic smile from a painterly perspective may be unknown or not known exactly enough for an algorithm to be invented for capturing them in a picture. Indeed, some would say that artistic, literary, or musical creativity can never be explicable in terms of algorithms.

Secondly, an algorithm exposes each and every step that must be followed. We can only construct an algorithm if its constitutive steps are in our conscious awareness. But so many of the actions we perform in riding a bicycle or grasping the nuances of a scene we wish to paint occur in what cognitive scientists call the 'cognitive unconscious'. There are limits to the extent such unconscious acts can be raised to the surface of consciousness.

Thirdly, even if we understand the nature of the task (reasonably) well, the task may involve multiple variables or parameters that interact with one another in nontrivial ways. Our knowledge or understanding of these interactions may be imperfect, incomplete, or hopelessly inadequate. The problem of designing a computer's outer architecture (see Chapter 5), for example, manifests this characteristic. The architect may well understand the actual parts that will go into an outer architecture (data types, operations, memory system, operand addressing modes, instruction formats, word length), but the range of variations for each such part, and the influences of these variations upon one another may be only inexactly or vaguely understood. Indeed, comprehending the full nature of these interactions may well exceed the architect's cognitive capacity.

Fourthly, even if one understands the problem well enough, and possesses knowledge about the problem domain, and can construct an algorithm to solve the problem, the amount of computational resources (time or space) needed to execute the algorithm may be simply infeasible. Algorithms of exponential time complexity (see Chapter 3) are examples.

Playing the game of chess is a case in point. The nature of the problem is very well understood. It has precise rules for legal moves, and is a game of 'perfect information' in the sense that each player can see all the pieces on the board at each point of time. The possible outcomes are precisely defined: White wins, Black wins, or they draw.

But consider the player's dilemma. Whenever it is his turn to play, his ideal objective is to choose a move that will lead to a win. In principle there is an optimum strategy (algorithm) the chess player can follow:

> The player whose turn it is to make the move considers all possible moves for himself. For each such move he then considers all

possible moves for the opponent; and for each of his opponent's possible moves, he considers again all his possible moves; and so on until an end state is reached: a win, a loss, or a draw. Then working backwards, the player determines whether the current position would force a win, and selects a move accordingly, assuming the opponent makes her moves most favourable to her.

This is called 'exhaustive search' or the 'brute force' method. In principle it will work. But of course, it is *impractical*. It has been estimated that in typical board configurations there are about thirty possible legal moves. Assume that a typical game lasts about forty moves before resignation by one of the players. Then beginning at the beginning, a player must consider thirty possible next moves; for each of these, there are thirty possible moves for the opponent, that is, 30^2 possibilities in the second move; for each of these 30^2 choices there are another thirty alternatives in the third move, that is, 30^3 possibilities. And so on until in the fortieth move the number of possibilities is 30^{40}. So at the very beginning, a player will have to consider $30 + 30^2 + 30^3 + 30^4 + \ldots + 30^{40}$ alternative moves before making an 'optimum' move. The space of alternative pathways is astronomically large.

Ultimately, if an algorithm is to be constructed to solve a problem, whatever knowledge is required about the problem for the algorithm to work *must be entirely embedded in the algorithm*. As we have noted in Chapter 3, an algorithm is a self-contained piece of procedural knowledge. To do a litmus test, perform a paper-and-pencil multiplication, evaluate the factorial of a number, generate reverse Polish expressions from infix arithmetic expressions (see Chapter 4)—all one needs to know is the algorithm itself. If one cannot incorporate any and all the necessary knowledge into the algorithm, there *is* no algorithm.

The world is full of tasks or problems manifesting the kinds of characteristics just mentioned. They include not just intellectual and creative work—scientific research, invention, designing, creative writing, mathematical work, literary analysis, historical research—but also the kinds of tasks professional practitioners—doctors, architects, engineers, industrial designers, planners, teachers, craftspeople—do. Even ordinary, humdrum activities—driving through a busy thoroughfare, making a decision about a job offer, planning a holiday trip—are not conducive to algorithmic solutions, or at least to efficient algorithmic solutions.

And yet, people go about performing these tasks and solving such problems. They do not wait for algorithms, efficient or otherwise. Indeed, if we had to wait for algorithms to solve any or all our problems then we, as a species, would have long been extinct. From an evolutionary point of view, algorithms are not all there is to our ways of thinking. And so the question arises: what other *computational* means are at our disposal to perform such tasks? The answer is to resort to a mode of computing that deploys *heuristics*.

Heuristics are rules, precepts, principles, hypotheses based on common sense, experience, judgement, analogies, informed guesses, etc., that offer promise but are not guaranteed to solve problems. We encountered heuristics in the last chapter in the discussion of computer architecture. However, to speak of computer architecture as a heuristics-based science of the artificial is one thing; to deploy heuristics in automatic computation is another. It is this latter, *heuristic computing*, that we now consider.

Search and ye *may* find

Heuristic computing embodies a spirit of adventure! There is an element of uncertainty and the unknown in heuristic computing. A problem solving agent (a human being or a computer) looking for a heuristic solution to a problem is, in effect, in a kind of *terra incognita*. And just as someone in an unknown physical territory goes into exploration or search mode so also the heuristic agent: he, she, or it *searches* for a solution to the problem, in what computer scientists call a *problem space*, never quite sure that a solution will obtain. Thus one kind of heuristic computing is also called *heuristic search*.

Consider, for example, the following scenario. You are entering a very large parking area attached to an auditorium where you wish to watch an event. The problem is to find a parking space. Cars are already parked there but you obviously have no knowledge of the distribution or location of empty spots. So what does one do?

In this case, the parking area is, literally, the problem space. And all you can do is, literally, search for an empty spot. But rather than searching aimlessly or randomly, you may decide to adopt a 'first fit' policy: pull into the first available empty spot you encounter. Or you may adopt a 'best fit' policy: find an empty spot that is the nearest to the auditorium.

These are heuristics that help *direct* the search through the problem space. There are tradeoffs, of course: the first fit strategy may reduce the search time but you may have to walk a long way to reach the auditorium; the best fit may demand a much longer search time, but if successful, the walk time may be relatively short. But, of course, *neither heuristic guarantees success*: neither is algorithmic in this sense. In both cases there may be no empty slot found, in which case you may either search indefinitely or you *terminate* the search by using a separate criterion, for example, 'exit if the search time exceeds a limit'.

Many strategies, however, that deploy heuristics have all the characteristics of an algorithm (as we discussed in Chapter 3)—with one notable difference: they give only 'nearly right' answers for a problem, or they may only give correct answers to some instances of the problem. Computer scientists, thus, refer to some kinds of heuristic problem solving techniques as *heuristic* or *approximate* algorithms, in which case we may need to distinguish them from what we may call *exact* algorithms. The term 'heuristic computing' encompasses both heuristic search and heuristic algorithms. An instance of the latter is presented shortly.

A meta-heuristic called 'satisficing'

Typically, in an optimization problem, the objective is to find the best possible solution to the problem. Many optimization problems have exact algorithmic solutions. Unfortunately, these algorithms are very often of exponential time complexity and so, impractical, even infeasible, to use for large instances of the problem. The chess problem considered earlier is an example. So what does a problem solver do, if optimal algorithms are computationally infeasible?

Instead of stubbornly pursuing the goal of optimality, the agent may aspire to achieve more feasible or 'reasonable' goals that are less than optimal but are 'acceptably good'. If a solution is obtained that meets this aspiration level then the problem solver is satisfied. Herbert Simon coined a term for this kind of mentality: *satisficing*. To satisfice is a more modest ambition than to optimize; it is to choose the feasible good over the infeasible best.

The satisficing principle is a very high level, very general, heuristic which can serve as a springboard for identifying more domain-specific heuristics. We may well call it a 'meta-heuristic'.

A chess-related satisficing heuristic. Consider the chess player's dilemma. As we have seen, optimal search is ruled out. More practical strategies are required, demanding the use of chess-related (domain-specific) heuristic principles. Among the simplest is the following.

Consider a chess board configuration (the positions of all the pieces currently on the board) **C**. Evaluate the 'promise' of **C** using some 'goodness' measure $G(\mathbf{C})$ which takes into account the general characteristics of $\mathbf{C}$ (the number and kinds of chess pieces, their relative positions, etc.).

Suppose $\mathbf{M1}$, $\mathbf{M2}, \ldots, \mathbf{Mn}$ are the moves that can be made by a player in configuration $\mathbf{C}$, and suppose the resulting configurations after each such move is $\mathbf{M1C}$, $\mathbf{M2C}$, etc. Then choose a move that maximizes the goodness value of the resulting configuration. That is, choose the $\mathbf{Mi}$ whose goodness value $G(\mathbf{MiC})$ is the highest.

Notice that there is a kind of optimality attempted here. But this is a 'local' or 'short-term' optimization, looking ahead just one move. It is not a very sophisticated heuristic, but it is of a kind that the casual chess player may cultivate. But it does demand a level of deep knowledge on the player's part (whether a human being or a computer) about the relative goodness of board configurations.

Chess playing exemplifies instances of satisficing heuristic search. Consider now an instance of a satisficing heuristic algorithm.

A heuristic algorithm

Recall the discussion of parallel processing in the last chapter. A pair of tasks Ti, Tj in a task stream (at whatever level of abstraction) can be processed in parallel providing Bernstein's data independency conditions are satisfied.

Consider now a sequential stream of machine instructions generated by a compiler for a target physical computer from a high level language sequential program (see Chapter 4). If, however, the target computer can execute instructions simultaneously then the compiler has one more task to perform: to identify parallelism between instructions in the instruction stream and produce a *parallel instruction stream*, where each element of this stream consists of a set of instructions that can be executed in parallel (call this a 'parallel set').

This is, in fact, an optimization problem if the goal is to minimize the number of parallel sets in the parallel instruction stream. An optimizing algorithm would entail, like the case of the chess problem, an exhaustive search strategy and thus be computationally impractical.

In practice, more satisficing heuristics are applied. An example is what I will call here the 'First Come, First Serve' (FCFS) algorithm.

Consider the following sequential instruction stream S. (For simplicity, there are no iterations or **goto**s in this example.)

I1: $A \leftarrow B$;
I2: $C \leftarrow D + E$;
I3: $B \leftarrow E + F - 1/W$;
I4: $Z \leftarrow C + Q$;
I5: $D \leftarrow A/X$;
I6: $R \leftarrow B - Q$;
I7: $S \leftarrow D * Z$.

The FCFS algorithm is as follows.

FCFS:

> **Input**: A straight line sequential instruction stream $S:$ < I1, I2,…, In>;
>
> **Output**: A straight line parallel instruction stream P consisting of a sequence of parallel sets of instructions each and every one of which are present in S.

For each successive instruction I in S starting with I1 and ending with In, place I in the earliest possible existing parallel set subject to Bernstein's data independency conditions. If this is not possible—because of data dependency precluding placing I in any of the existing parallel sets—a new (empty) parallel set is created *after* the existing ones and I is placed there.

When this FCFS algorithm is applied to the earlier example it can be seen that the output is the parallel instruction stream P:

I1 || I2;
I3 || I4 || I5;
I6 || I7.

Here, '||' symbolizes parallel processing, and ';' sequential processing. This is, then, a parallel stream of three parallel sets of instructions.

FCFS is a satisficing strategy. It places each instruction in the earliest possible parallel set so that succeeding data dependent instructions can also appear as early as possible in the parallel stream. The satisficing criterion is: 'Examine each instruction on its own merit relative to its predecessors and ignore what follows'. For this particular example, FCFS produces an optimal output (a minimal sequence of parallel sets). However, there may well be other input streams for which FCFS will produce suboptimal parallel sets.

So, what is the difference between exact and heuristic algorithms? In the former case the 'goodness' is judged by evaluating its time (or space) complexity. There is no surprise or uncertainty attached to the outputs. Two or more exact algorithms for the same task (such as to solve systems of algebraic equations, sort files of data in ascending sequence, process payrolls, or compute the GCD of two integers, etc.) will not vary in their outputs; they will (or may) differ only in their performances and in their respective aesthetic appeal. In the case of heuristic algorithms there is more to the story. The algorithms may certainly be compared for their relative time complexities. (FCFS is an $\mathbf{O}(n^2)$ algorithm for an input stream of size n.) But they may also be compared in terms of their outputs since the outputs may occasion surprise. Two parallelism detection algorithms or two chess programs employing different sets of heuristics may yield different results.

And how they differ is an empirical issue. One must implement the algorithms as executable programs, conduct experiments on various test data, examine the outputs, and ascertain their strengths and weaknesses based on the experiments. Heuristic computing, thus, entails experimentation.

Heuristics and artificial intelligence

Artificial intelligence (AI) is a branch of computer science concerned with the theory, design and implementation of computational artefacts that perform tasks we normally associate with human thinking: such artefacts can be viewed then as 'possessing' artificial intelligence. Thus it provides a bridge between computer science and psychology. And one of the earliest reflections on the possibility of artificial intelligence was due to electrical engineer Claude Shannon in the late 1940s when he considered the idea of programming a computer to play chess. In fact, ever since, computer chess has remained a significant focus in AI research. However, the most influential manifesto of what became AI (the term itself was coined by one of the pioneers of the subject, John McCarthy, in the mid-1950s) was a provocative article by Alan Turing (of Turing machine reputation) in 1950 who posed and proposed an answer to the question: 'What does it mean to claim that a computer can think?' His answer involved a kind of experiment—a 'thought experiment'—in which a human being asks questions of two invisible agents through some 'neutral' communication means (so that the interrogator cannot guess the identity of the responder from the means of response), one of the agents being a person, the other a computer. If the interrogator cannot correctly guess the identity of the computer as responder more than, say 40 per cent–50 per cent of the time then the computer may be regarded as manifesting human-like intelligence. This test came to be called the *Turing Test*, and was for some years a holy grail of AI research.

AI is a vast area and there is, in fact, more than one *paradigm* favoured by AI researchers. (I use the word 'paradigm' in philosopher of science Thomas Kuhn's sense.) Here, however, to illuminate further the scope and power of heuristic computing, I will consider only the *heuristic search paradigm* in AI.

This paradigm concerns itself with intelligent agents—natural and artificial: humans and machines. And it rests on two hypotheses articulated most explicitly by Allen Newell and Herbert Simon, the originators of the paradigm:

> *Physical Symbol System Hypothesis*: A physical symbol system has the necessary and sufficient means for general intelligent action.
>
> *Heuristic Search Hypothesis*: A physical symbol system solves problems by progressively and selectively (heuristically) searching through a problem space of symbol structures.

By 'physical symbol system', Newell and Simon meant systems that process symbol structures and yet are grounded in a physical substrate—what I have called material and liminal computational artefacts, except that they include both natural and artificial objects under their rubric.

A very general picture of a heuristic search-based problem solving agent (human or artificial) is depicted in Figure 8. A problem is solved by first creating a symbolic representation of the problem in a working memory or *problem space*. The problem representation will typically denote the *initial state*, which is where the agent starts, and the *goal state*, which represents a solution to the problem. In addition, the problem space must be capable of representing all possible states that might be reached in the effort

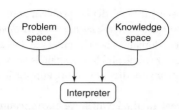

8. General structure of a heuristic search system.

to go from the initial to the goal state. The problem space is what mathematicians might call a 'state space'.

Transitions from one state to another are effected by appealing to the contents of the agent's *knowledge space* (the contents of a long-term memory). Elements from this knowledge space are selected and applied to a 'current state' in the problem space resulting in a new state. The organ that does this is shown in Figure 8 as the *interpreter* (on which more later). The successive applications of knowledge elements in effect result in the agent conducting a *search* for a solution through the problem space. This search process constitutes a computation. The problem is solved when, beginning with the initial state, the application of a sequence of knowledge elements results in the goal state being reached.

However, since a problem space may be arbitrarily large, the search through it is not randomly conducted. Rather, the agent deploys heuristics to control the amount of search, to prune away parts of the search space as unnecessary, and thereby converge to a solution as rapidly as possible.

Weak methods and strong methods

The heart of the heuristic search paradigm is, thus, the heuristics contained in the knowledge space. These may range from the very general—applicable to a wide range of problem domains—to the very specific—relevant to particular problem domains. The former are called *weak methods* and the latter *strong methods*. In general, when the problem domain is poorly understood weak methods are more promising; when the problem domain is known or understood in more detail strong methods are more appropriate.

One effective weak method (which we have encountered several times already) is *divide-and-rule*. Another is called *means-ends analysis*:

> Given a current problem state and a goal state, determine the
> difference between the two. Then reduce the difference by applying
> a relevant 'operator'. If, however, the necessary precondition for
> the operator to apply is not satisfied, reduce the difference between
> the current state and the precondition by recursively applying
> means-ends analysis to the pair, current state and precondition.

An example of a problem to which both divide-and-conquer and means-ends analysis can apply together is that of a student planning her degree program. Divide-and-conquer decomposes the problem into subproblems corresponding to each of the years of the degree program. The original goal state (to graduate in a particular subject in X number of years, say) is decomposed into 'subgoal' states for each of the X years. For each year, the student will identify the initial state for that year (the courses already taken before that year) and attempt to identify courses to be taken that eliminate the difference between the initial and goal states for that year. The search for courses is narrowed by selecting those that are mandatory. But some of these courses may require prerequisites. Thus means-ends analysis is applied to reduce the gap between the initial state and the prerequisites. And so on.

Notice that means-ends analysis is a *recursive* strategy (see Chapter 3). So what is so 'heuristic' about it? The point is that there is no guarantee that in a particular problem domain, means-ends analysis will terminate successfully. For example, given a current state and a goal state, several actions may be applicable to reduce the difference. The action chosen may determine the difference between success and failure.

Strong methods usually represent *expert knowledge* of the kind specialists in a problem domain possess through formal education, hands-on training, and experience. Computational systems that determine the molecular structure of chemicals or aid engineers in their design projects are typical instances. These heuristics are often represented in the knowledge space as rules (called *productions*) of the form:

IF condition THEN action.

That is, if the current state in the problem space matches the 'condition' part of a production then the corresponding 'action' *may* be taken. As an example from the domain of digital circuit design (and implemented as part of a heuristic design automation system):

IF   the goal of the circuit module is to convert a serial signal to a
       parallel one
THEN use a shift register.

It is possible that the current state in the problem space is such that it matches the condition parts of several productions:

IF condition1 THEN action1;
IF condition2 THEN action2.
            ....
IF condition*M* THEN action*M*.

In such a situation the choice of an action to take may have to be guided by a higher level heuristic (e.g. select the first matching production). This may turn out to be a wrong choice as realized later in the computation, in which case the system must 'backtrack' to a prior state and explore some other production.

Interpreting heuristic rules

Notice the 'interpreter' in Figure 8. Its task is to execute a cyclic algorithm analogous to the ICycle in a physical computer (Chapter 5):

Match: Identify all the productions in the knowledge space the condition parts of which match the current state in the problem space. Collect these rules into a *conflict set*.

Select a preferred rule from the conflict set according to a selection heuristic.

Execute the action part of the preferred rule.
Goto Match.

Apart from the uncertainty associated with the heuristic search paradigm, the other noticeable difference from algorithms (exact or heuristic) is (as mentioned before) that in the latter all the knowledge required to execute an algorithm is embedded in the algorithm itself. In contrast, in the heuristic search paradigm almost all the knowledge is located in the knowledge space (or long-term memory). The complexity of the heuristic search paradigm lies mostly in the richness of the knowledge space.

Chapter 7
Computational thinking

A certain mentality

Most sciences in the modern era—say, after the Second World War—are so technical, indeed esoteric, that their deeper comprehension remains largely limited to the specialists, the community of those sciences' practitioners. Think, for example, of the modern physics of fundamental particles. At best, when relevant, their implications are revealed to the larger public by way of technological consequences.

Yet there are some sciences that touch the imagination of those outside the specialists by way of the compelling nature of their central ideas. The theory of evolution is one such instance from the realm of the natural sciences. Its tentacles of influence have extended into the reaches of sociology, psychology, economics, and even computer science, fields of thought having nothing to do with genes or natural selection.

Among the sciences of the artificial, computer science manifests a similar characteristic. I am not referring to the ubiquitous and 'in your face' technological tools which have colonized the social world. I am referring, rather, to the emergence of a certain *mentality*.

This mentality, or at least its promise, was articulated passionately and eloquently by one of the pioneers of artificial intelligence, Seymour Papert, in his book *Mindstorms* (1980). His aim in this work, Papert announced, was to discuss and describe how the computer might afford human beings new ways of learning and thinking, not only as a practical, instrumental artefact but in much more fundamental, conceptual ways. Such influences would facilitate modes of thinking even when the thinkers were not in direct contact with the physical machine. For Papert, the computer held promise as a potential 'carrier of powerful ideas and of seeds of cultural change'. His book, he promised, would speak of how the computer could help humans fruitfully transgress the traditional boundaries separating objective knowledge and self-knowledge, and between the humanities and the sciences.

What Papert was articulating was a vision, perhaps utopian, that went well beyond the purely instrumental influence of computers and computing in the affairs of the world. This latter vision had existed from the very beginnings of automatic computation in the time of Charles Babbage and Ada, Countess of Lovelace in the mid-19th century. Papert's vision, rather, was the inculcation of a mentality that would guide, shape, and influence the ways in which a person would think about, perceive, and respond to, aspects of the world—one's inner world and the world outside—which prima facie have no apparent connection to computing—perhaps by way of analogy, metaphor, and imagination.

Over a quarter of a century after Papert's manifesto, computer scientist Jeanette Wing gave this mentality a name: *computational thinking*. But Wing's vision is perhaps more prosaic than was Papert's. Computational thinking, she wrote in 2008, entails approaches to such activities as problem solving, designing, and making sense of intelligent behaviour that draws on fundamental concepts of computing. Yet computational thinking cannot be an island of its own. In the realm of problem solving it would be akin to mathematical thinking; in the domain of design it would share features with the engineering mentality; and in understanding intelligent systems (including, of course, the mind) it might find common ground with scientific thinking.

Like Papert, Wing disassociated the mentality of computational thinking from the physical computer itself: one can think computationally without the presence of a computer.

But what does this mentality of computational thinking entail? We will see some examples later but before that let us follow AI researcher Paul Rosenbloom's interpretation of the notion of computational thinking in terms of two kinds of relationships: one is *interaction*, a concept introduced earlier (see Chapter 2) to mean, in Rosenbloom's phrase, 'reciprocal action, effect or influence' between two entities. However, interaction can signify unidirectional influence of one system A on another system B (notationally, Rosenbloom depicted this as '$A \rightarrow B$' or '$B \leftarrow A$') as well as bidirectional or mutual influence (notationally '$A \leftarrow \rightarrow B$'). By *implementation* Rosenbloom meant to 'put into effect' a system A at a higher abstraction level in terms of interacting processes within a system B at a lower level of abstraction (notationally, 'A/B'). A special case of implementation is *simulation*: B simulates A (A/B) when B acts to imitate or mimic the behaviour of A.

Using these two relationships, Rosenbloom explained, the simplest representation of computational thinking is when a computational artefact (C) influences the behaviour of a human being (H): C $\rightarrow$ H. Rosenbloom then goes further. Instead of just a human being H, suppose we consider a human simulating a computational artefact C: C/H. In this case we have the relationship C $\rightarrow$ C/H, meaning that computational artefacts influence human beings who simulate the behaviour of such artefacts. Or we may go still further: consider a human being H simulating mentally a computational artefact C which itself has implemented or is simulating the behaviour of some real world domain D: D/C/H. For example, suppose D is human behaviour. Then D/C means using a computer to simulate or model human behaviour. And D/C/H means a human being mentally simulating such a computer model of human behaviour. This leads to the following interpretation of computational thinking: C → D/C/H.

More nuanced interpretations are possible, but these interpretations in terms of interaction and implementation/simulation suffice to illustrate the general scope of computational thinking.

Computational thinking as mental skills

The most obvious influence computing can exercise on people is as a source of mental skills: a repertoire of analytical and problem solving tools which humans can apply in the course of their lives regardless of the presence or absence of actual computers. This was what Jeanette Wing had in mind. In particular, she took abstraction as the 'essence', the 'nuts and bolts' of computational thinking. But while (as we have seen throughout this book) abstraction is undoubtedly a core computational concept, computer science offers many more notions that one may assimilate and integrate into one's kit of thinking tools. I am thinking of heuristic methods, weak and strong; the idea of satisficing rather than optimizing as a realistic decision-making objective; of thinking in algorithmic terms and comprehending when and whether this is the appropriate pathway to problem solving; of the conditions and architecture of parallel processing as means for approaching multitasking endeavours; of approaching a problem situation from the 'top down' (beginning with the goal and the initial problem state, and refining the goal into simpler subgoals, and the latter into still simpler subgoals, etc.) or 'bottom up' (beginning with the goal and the lowest level building blocks and constructing a solution by composing building blocks into larger building blocks, and so on). But what is significant is that to acquire these tools of thought demands a certain level of mastery of the concepts of computer science. For Wing this entails introducing computational thinking as part of the educational curriculum from an early age.

But computational thinking entails more than analytical and problem solving skills. It encompasses a way of *imagining*, by way of seeing analogies and constructing metaphors. It is this *combination* of technical skills and imagination that, I think, Papert had in mind, and which provides the full richness of the mentality of computational thinking. We consider now some realms of intellectual and scientific inquiry where this mentality has proved to be effective.

Thinking computationally about the mind

Certainly, one of the most potent, albeit controversial, manifestations of this mentality is in thinking about thinking: the influence of computer science on cognitive psychology. Turning Turing's celebrated question—whether computers can think (the basis of AI)—on its head, cognitive psychologists consider the question: Is thinking a computational process?

The response to this question reaches back to the pioneering work of Allan Newell and Herbert Simon in the late 1950s, in their development of an information processing theory of human problem solving which combined such computational issues as heuristics, levels of abstraction, and symbol structures with logic. Much more recently it has led to the construction of models of *cognitive architecture*, most prominently by researchers such as psychologist John Anderson and computer scientists Allen Newell, John Laird, and Paul Rosenbloom. Anderson's series of models, called, generically, ACT, and that of Newell et al. called SOAR, were both strongly influenced by the basic principles of inner computer architecture (see Chapter 5). In these models the architecture of cognition is explored in terms of memory hierarchies holding symbol structures that represent aspects of the world, and the manipulation and processing of symbol structures by processes analogous to the instruction interpretation cycle (ICycle). These architectural models have been extensively investigated both theoretically and empirically as possible theories of the thinking mind at a certain abstraction level. Another kind of computationally influenced model of the mind begins with the principles of parallel processing and distributed computing, and envisions mind as a 'society' of distributed, communicating, and interacting cognitive modules. An influential proponent of this kind of mental modelling was AI pioneer Marvin Minsky. As for cognitive scientist and philosopher Margaret Boden, she titled her magisterial history of cognitive science *Mind as Machine* (2006): the mind *is* a computational device, by her account.

The computational brain

Representing or modelling the neuronal structure of the brain as a computational system and, conversely, computational artefacts as networks of highly abstract neuron-like entities has a history that reaches back to the pioneering work of mathematician Warren Pitts and neurophysiologist Warren McCulloch, and the irrepressible John von Neumann in the 1940s. Over the next sixty years a scientific paradigm called *connectionism* has evolved. In this approach, the mentality of computational thinking is expressed most specifically in the design of highly interconnected networks (hence the term 'connectionism') of very simple computational elements which collectively serve to model the behaviour of basic brain processes that are the building blocks in higher cognitive processes (such as detecting cues or recognizing patterns in visual processes). Connectionist architectures of the brain are at a lower abstraction level than the symbol processing cognitive architectures mentioned in the previous section.

The emergence of cognitive science

Symbol processing cognitive architectures of mind and connectionist models of the brain are two of the ways in which computational artefacts and the principles of computer science have influenced the shaping and emergence of the relatively new interdisciplinary field of *cognitive science*. I must emphasize that not all cognitive scientists—for instance the psychologist Jerome Bruner—take computation to be a central element of cognition. Nonetheless, the idea of understanding such activities as thinking, remembering, planning, problem solving, decision making, perceiving, and conceptualizing and understanding by way of constructing computational models and computation-based hypotheses is a compelling one; in particular, the view of computer science as a science of automatic symbol processing served as a powerful *catalyst* in the emergence of cognitive science itself. The core of Margaret Boden's history of cognitive science, mentioned in the previous section, is the development of automatic computing.

Understanding human creativity

The fascinating subject of creativity, ranging from the exceptional, historically original kind to the personal, everyday brand, is a vast topic that has attracted the professional attention of psychologists, psychoanalysts, philosophers, pedagogues, aestheticians, art theorists, design theorists, and intellectual historians and biographers; not to speak of the more self-reflexive creators themselves (scientists, inventors, poets and writers, musicians, artists, etc.). The range of approaches to, models and theories of, creativity is, accordingly, bewilderingly large, not least because of the many definitions of creativity.

But at least one community of creativity researchers has resorted to computational thinking as a *modus operandi*. They have proposed computational models and theories of the creative process that draw heavily on the principles of heuristic computing, representation of knowledge as complex symbol structures (called schemas), and the principles of abstraction. Here too, such is its compelling influence, computational thinking has afforded a common ground for the analysis of scientific, technological, artistic, literary, and musical creativity: a marriage of many cultures as Papert had hoped for.

For example, literary scholar Mark Turner has applied computational principles to the problem of understanding literary composition, just as philosopher of science and cognitive scientist Paul Thagard strove to explain scientific revolutions by way of computational models, and the present author, a computer scientist and creativity researcher, constructed a computational explanation for the design and invention of technological artefacts and ideas in the artificial sciences. The mentality of computational thinking has served as the glue that binds these different intellectual and creative cultures into one. In many of these computational studies of creativity, computer science has provided a precision of thought in which to express concepts pertaining to creativity which was formerly absent.

To take an example, the writer Arthur Koestler in his monumental work *The Act of Creation* (1964) postulated a process called 'bisociation' as the mechanism by which creative acts are effected. By bisociation, Koestler meant the coming together of two or more unconnected concepts and their blending, resulting in an original product. However, precisely how bisociation occurred remained unexplained. Computational thinking has afforded some creativity researchers (such as Mark Turner and this writer) explanations of certain bisociations in the precise language of computer science.

Understanding molecular information processing

In 1953, James Watson and Francis Crick famously discovered the structure of the DNA molecule. Thus was initiated the science of molecular biology. Its concerns included understanding and discovering such mechanisms as the replication of DNA, transcription of DNA to RNA, and translation of RNA into protein—fundamental biological processes. Thus the notion of molecules as carriers of information entered the biological consciousness. Theoretical biologists influenced by computational ideas began to model genetical processes in computational terms (which, incidentally, also led to the invention of algorithms based on genetical concepts). Computational thinking shaped what was called 'biological information processing' or, in contemporary jargon, *bioinformatics*.

Epilogue: is computer science a universal science?

Throughout this book the premise has been that computer science is a science of the artificial: that it is centred on symbol processing (or computational) artefacts; that it is a science of how things ought to be rather than how things are; that the goals of the artificers (algorithm designers, programmers, software engineers, computer architects, informaticists) must be taken into account in understanding the nature of this science. In all these respects the distinction from the natural sciences is clear.

However, in the last chapter we have seen that computational thinking serves as a bridge between the world of computational artefacts and the natural world, specifically, that of biological molecules, human cognition, and neuronal processes. Could it be, then, that computing not only affords a mentality but that, more insidiously, computation as a phenomenon embraces the natural and the artificial? That computer science is a *universal* science?

In recent years some computer scientists have thought precisely along these lines. Thus, Peter Denning has argued that computing should no longer be thought of as a science of the artificial, since information processes are abundantly found in nature. Denning and another computer scientist, Peter Freeman, have contended that in the past few decades the focus of (some computer scientists') attention has shifted from computational artefacts to information processes per se—including natural processes.

For Denning, Freeman, and yet another computer scientist Richard Snodgrass, computing is, thus, a *natural* science since computer scientists are as much in the business of discovering *how things are* (in the brain, in the living cell, and, even, in the realm of computational artefacts) as in elucidating how things ought to be. This point of view implies that computational artefacts are of the same ontological category as natural entities; or that there is no distinction to be made between the natural and the artificial. Snodgrass, in fact, invented a word to describe the natural science of computer science: 'Ergalics', from the Greek root 'ergon' ($\epsilon\rho\gamma\omega\nu$), meaning 'work'.

Paul Rosenbloom, in broad agreement with Snodgrass, but wishing to avoid a neologism, simply identified the computer *sciences* alongside the physical, life, and social sciences, as the 'fourth great scientific domain'.

The uniqueness of computer science as constituting a paradigm of its own has been an abiding theme of this book, and so Rosenbloom's thesis is consistent with this theme. The question is whether one should distinguish between the study of *natural information* processes and that of *artificial symbolic* processes. Here, the distinction between information and symbol seems justified. In the natural domain, entities do not represent anything but themselves. Entities such as neurons, or the nucleotides that are the building blocks of DNA, or the amino acids constituting proteins, do not represent anything but themselves. Thus, I find it problematic to refer to DNA processing as *symbol* processing, though to refer to these entities as carriers of non-referential *information* seems valid.

Ontologically, I think, a distinction has to be made between computer science as a science of the artificial and computer science as a natural science. In the former, human agency (in the form of goals and purpose, accessing knowledge, effecting action) is part of the science. In the latter case, agency is avowedly absent. The paradigms are fundamentally distinct.

Be that as it may, and regardless of any such possible ontological difference, what computer science has given us, as the preceding chapters have tried to show, is a remarkably distinctive way of perceiving, thinking about, and solving a breathtakingly broad spectrum of problems—spanning natural, social, cultural, technological, and economic realms. This is surely its most *original* scientific contribution to the modern world.

Further reading

The reader may wish to study the topics of the various chapters in more depth. The following list is a mix of some classic and historically influential (and still eminently readable) works and more contemporary texts; a mix of essays and historical works written for a broad readership and somewhat more technical articles.

Preface

S. Dasgupta (2014). *It Began with Babbage: The Genesis of Computer Science*. New York: Oxford University Press: esp. chapter 15.

Chapter 1: The 'stuff' of computing

S. Dasgupta (2014). *It Began with Babbage: The Genesis of Computer Science*. New York: Oxford University Press: chapters 1 & 2.

L. Floridi (2010). *Information: A Very Short Introduction*. Oxford: Oxford University Press.

D. Ince (2011). *Computer: A Very Short Introduction*. Oxford: Oxford University Press.

D.E. Knuth (1996). 'Algorithms, Programs and Computer Science' (originally published in 1966). *Selected Papers in Computer Science*. Stanford, CA: Center for the Study of Language and Information.

A. Newell, A.J. Perlis, & H.A. Simon (1967). 'What is Computer Science?' *Science*, 157, 1373–4.

A. Newell & H.A. Simon (1976). 'Computer Science as Empirical Inquiry: Symbols and Search', *Communications of the ACM*, 19, 113–26.

P.S. Rosenbloom (2010). *On Computing: The Fourth Great Scientific Domain*. Cambridge, MA: MIT Press.

Chapter 2: Computational artefacts

C.G. Bell, J.C. Mudge, & J.E. McNamara (1978). 'Seven Views of Computer Systems', pp. 1–26, in C.G. Bell, J.C. Mudge, & J.E. McNamara (ed.). *Computer Engineering: A DEC View of Hardware Systems Design*. Bedford, MA: Digital Press.

C.G. Bell, D.P. Siweorek, & A. Newell (1982). *Computer Structures: Principles and Examples*. New York: McGraw-Hill: esp. chapter 2.

S. Dasgupta (2014). *It Began with Babbage: The Genesis of Computer Science*. New York: Oxford University Press: esp. prologue and chapter 4.

J. Copeland (ed.) (2004). *The Essential Turing*. Oxford: Oxford University Press.

J. Copeland (2004). 'Computing', pp. 3–18, in L. Floridi (ed.). *Philosophy of Computing and Information*. Oxford: Blackwell.

E.W. Dijkstra (1968). 'The Structure of "THE" Multiprogramming System', *Communications of the ACM*, 11, 341–6.

E.W. Dijkstra (1971). 'Hierarchical Ordering of Sequential Processes', *Acta Informatica*, 1, 115–38.

D. Ince (2011). *The Computer: A Very Short Introduction*. Oxford: Oxford University Press.

H.H. Pattee (ed.) (1973). *Hierarchy Theory: The Challenge of Complex Systems*. New York: Braziller.

H.A. Simon (1996). *The Sciences of the Artificial* (3rd edn). Cambridge, MA: MIT Press.

A.S. Tanenbaum & H. Bos (2014). *Modern Operating Systems* (4th edn). Englewood Cliffs, NJ: Prentice-Hall.

Chapter 3: Algorithmic thinking

J. Copeland (2004). 'Computing', pp. 3–18, in L. Floridi (ed.). *Philosophy of Computing and Information*. Oxford: Blackwell.

E.W. Dijkstra (1965). 'Programming Considered as a Human Activity', *Proceedings of the 1965 IFIP Congress*. Amsterdam: North-Holland, pp. 213–17.

D.E. Knuth (1996). 'Algorithms', pp. 59–86, in D.E. Knuth. *Selected Papers on Computer Science*. Stanford, CA: Center for the Study of Language and Information.

D.E. Knuth (1997). *The Art of Computer Programming. Volume 1. Fundamental Algorithms* (3rd edn). Reading, MA: Addison-Wesley.

D.E. Knuth (2001). 'Aesthetics', pp. 91–138, in D.E. Knuth. *Things a Computer Scientist Rarely Talks About*. Stanford, CA: Center for the Study of Language and Information.

R. Sedgewick & K. Wayne (2011). *Algorithms* (4th edn). Reading, MA: Addison-Wesley.

Chapter 4: The art, science, and engineering of programming

F.P. Brooks, Jr (1975). *The Mythical Man-Month: Essays on Software Engineering*. Reading, MA: Addison-Wesley.

P. Freeman (1987). *Software Perspectives*. Reading, MA: Addison-Wesley.

C.A.R. Hoare (1985). *The Mathematics of Programming*. Oxford: Clarendon Press.

C.A.R. Hoare (2006). 'The Ideal of Program Correctness'. <http://www.bcs.org/upload/pdf/correctness.pdf>. Retrieved 28 May 2014.

D.E. Knuth (1992). *Literate Programming*. Stanford, CA: Center for the Study of Language and Information. See esp. 'Computer Programming as Art', pp. 1–16.

D.E. Knuth (2001). *Things a Computer Scientist Rarely Talks About*. Stanford, CA: Center for the Study of Language and Information. See esp. 'Aesthetics', pp. 91–138.

I. Sommerville (2010). *Software Engineering* (9th edn). Reading, MA: Addison-Wesley.

M.V. Wilkes (1995). *Computing Perspectives*. San Francisco: Morgan Kauffman. Esp. 'Software and the Programmer', pp. 87–92; 'From FORTRAN and ALGOL to Object-Oriented Languages', pp. 93–101.

N. Wirth (1973). *Systematic Programming: An Introduction*. Englewood Cliffs, NJ: Prentice Hall.

Chapter 5: The discipline of computer architecture

G.S. Almasi & A. Gottlieb (1989). *Highly Parallel Computing*. New York: The Benjamin Cummings Publishing Company.

C.G. Bell, J.C. Mudge, & J.E. McNamara (ed.) (1978). *Computer Engineering: A DEC View of Hardware Systems Design*. Bedford, MA: Digital Press.

C.G. Bell, D.P. Sieweorek, & A. Newell (1982). *Computer Structures: Principles and Examples*. New York: McGraw-Hill.

S. Dasgupta (2014). *It Began with Babbage: The Genesis of Computer Science*. New York: Oxford University Press.

S. Habib (ed.) (1988). *Microprogramming and Firmware Engineering Methods*. New York: Van Nostrand Reinhold.

C. Hamacher, Z. Vranesic, & S. Zaky (2011). *Computer Organization and Embedded Systems* (5th edn). New York: McGraw-Hill.

K. Hwang & F.A. Briggs (1984). *Computer Architecture and Parallel Processing*. New York: McGraw-Hill.

D.E. Ince (2011). *The Computer: A Very Short Introduction*. Oxford: Oxford University Press.

D.A. Patterson & J.L. Henessy (2011). *Computer Architecture: A Quantitative Approach* (5th edn). Burlington, MA: Morgan Kaufmann.

A.S. Tanenbaum (2011). *Structured Computer Organization* (6th edn). Englewood Cliffs, NJ: Prentice Hall.

Chapter 6: Heuristic computing

D.R. Hofstadter (1999). *Gödel, Escher, Bach: An Eternal Golden Braid* (20th anniversary edn). New York: Basic Books.

A. Newell & H.A. Simon (1972). *Human Problem Solving*. Englewood Cliffs, NJ: Prentice Hall.

A. Newell & H.A. Simon (1976). 'Computer Science as Empirical Inquiry: Symbols and Search', *Communications of the ACM*, 19, 113–26.

J. Pearl (1984). *Heuristics: Intelligent Search Strategies for Computer Problem Solving*. Reading, MA: Addison-Wesley.

G. Polya & J.H. Conway (2014). *How to Solve It: A New Aspect of Mathematical Method*. Princeton, NJ: Princeton University Press. (Originally published in 1949).

D.L. Poole & A.K. Mackworth (2010). *Artificial Intelligence: Foundations of Computational Agents*. Cambridge: Cambridge University Press.

S. Russell & P. Norvig (2014). *Artificial Intelligence: A Modern Approach* (3rd edn). New Delhi: Dorling Kinderseley/Pearson.

H.A. Simon (1995). 'Artificial Intelligence: An Empirical Science', *Artificial Intelligence* 77, 1, 95–127.

H.A. Simon (1996). *The Sciences of the Artificial* (3rd edn). Cambridge, MA: MIT Press.

Chapter 7: Computational thinking

M.A. Boden (2006). *Minds as Machines. Volume 1.* Oxford: Clarendon Press.

S. Dasgupta (1994). *Creativity in Invention and Design: Computational and Cognitive Explorations of Technological Originality.* New York: Cambridge University Press.

S. Papert (1980). *Mindstorms.* New York: Basic Books.

P.S. Rosenbloom (2013). *On Computing: The Fourth Great Scientific Domain.* Cambridge, MA: MIT Press.

J. Searle (1984). *Minds, Brains and Science.* Cambridge, MA: Harvard University Press.

J. Setubal & J. Meidinis (1997). *Introduction to Computational Molecular Biology.* Pacific Grove, CA: Brooks/Cole Publishing Company.

C.A. Stewart (ed.) (2004). '*Bioinformatics:* Transforming Biomedical Research and Medical Care' [Special Section on Bioinformatics], *Communications of the ACM*, 47/11, 30–72.

P.R. Thagard (1988). *Computational Philosophy of Science.* Cambridge, MA: MIT Press.

P.R. Thagard (1992). *Conceptual Revolutions.* Princeton, NJ: Princeton University Press.

J.M. Wing (2006). 'Computational Thinking', *Communications of the ACM*, 49/3, 33–5.

J.M. Wing (2008). 'Computational Thinking and Thinking about Computing', *Philosophical Transactions of the Royal Society*, Series A, 366, pp. 3717–25.

Epilogue: is computer science a universal science?

S. Dasgupta (2014). *It Began with Babbage: The Genesis of Computer Science.* New York: Oxford University Press.

P.J. Denning & C.H. Martell (2015). *Great Principles of Computing.* Cambridge, MA: MIT Press.

P.J. Denning (2005). 'Is Computer Science Science?' *Communications of the ACM*, 48/4, 27–31.

P.J. Denning & P.A. Freeman (2009). 'Computing's Paradigm', *Communications of the ACM*, 52/12, 28–30.

P.S. Rosenbloom (2013). *On Computing: The Fourth Great Scientific Domain*. Cambridge, MA: MIT Press.

R. Snodgrass (2010). 'Ergalics: A Natural Science of Computing'. <http://citeseerx.ist.psu.edu/viewdoc/download?doi= 10.1.1.180.4704&rep=rep1&type=pdf>. Retrieved 16 Sept. 2015.

Index

P

R

S

Index

SOCIAL MEDIA
Very Short Introduction

Join our community

www.oup.com/vsi

- Join us online at the official Very Short Introductions **Facebook** page.
- Access the thoughts and musings of our authors with our online **blog**.
- Sign up for our monthly **e-newsletter** to receive information on all new titles publishing that month.
- Browse the full range of Very Short Introductions online.
- Read **extracts** from the Introductions for free.
- Visit our library of **Reading Guides**. These guides, written by our expert authors will help you to question again, why you think what you think.
- If you are a teacher or lecturer you can order inspection copies quickly and simply via our website.

Contents

Poems

Emily Dickinson

67

Success is counted sweetest
By those who ne'er succeed.
To comprehend a nectar
Requires sorest need.

Not one of all the purple Host
Who took the Flag today
Can tell the definition
So clear of Victory

As he defeated – dying –
On whose forbidden ear
The distant strains of triumph
Burst agonized and clear!

187

How many times these low feet staggered –
Only the soldered mouth can tell –
Try – can you stir the awful rivet –
Try – can you lift the hasps of steel!

Stroke the cool forehead – hot so often –
Lift – if you care – the listless hair –
Handle the adamantine fingers
Never a thimble – more – shall wear –

Buzz the dull flies – on the chamber window –
Brave – shines the sun through the freckled pane –
Fearless – the cobweb swings from the ceiling –
Indolent Housewife – in Daisies – lain!

193

I shall know why – when Time is over –
And I have ceased to wonder why –
Christ will explain each separate anguish
In the fair schoolroom of the sky –

He will tell me what "Peter" promised –
And I – for wonder at his woe –
I shall forget the drop of Anguish
That scalds me now – that scalds me now!

199

I'm "wife" – I've finished that –
That other state –
I'm Czar – I'm "Woman" now –
It's safer so –

How odd the Girl's life looks
Behind this soft Eclipse –
I think that Earth feels so
To folks in Heaven – now –

This being comfort – then
That other kind – was pain –
But why compare?
I'm "Wife"! Stop there!

211

Come slowly – Eden!
Lips unused to Thee –
Bashful – sip thy Jessamines –
As the fainting Bee –

Reaching late his flower,
Round her chamber hums –
Counts his nectars –
Enters – and is lost in Balms.

214

I taste a liquor never brewed –
From Tankards scooped in Pearl –
Not all the Vats upon the Rhine
Yield such an Alcohol!

Inebriate of Air – am I –
And Debauchee of Dew –
Reeling – thro endless summer days –
From inns of Molten Blue –

When 'Landlords' turn the drunken Bee
Out of the Foxglove's door –
When Butterflies – renounce their "drams" –
I shall but drink the more!

Till Seraphs swing their snowy Hats
And Saints – to windows run –
To see the little Tippler
Leaning against the – Sun –

216

Safe in their Alabaster Chambers –
Untouched by Morning
And untouched by Noon –
Sleep the meek members of the Resurrection –
Rafter of satin,
And Roof of stone.

Light laughs the breeze
In her Castle above them –
Babbles the Bee in a stolid Ear,
Pipe the Sweet Birds in ignorant cadence –
Ah, what sagacity perished here!

VERSION OF 1859

Safe in their Alabaster Chambers –
Untouched by Morning –
And untouched by Noon –
Lie the meek members of the Resurrection –
Rafter of Satin – and Roof of Stone!

Grand go the Years – in the Crescent – above them –
Worlds scoop their Arcs –
And Firmaments – row –
Diadems – drop – and Doges – surrender –
Soundless as dots – on a Disc of Snow –

VERSION OF 1861

225

Jesus! thy Crucifix
Enable thee to guess
The smaller size!

6

Jesus! thy second face
Mind thee in Paradise
Of ours!

228

Blazing in Gold and quenching in Purple
Leaping like Leopards to the Sky
Then at the feet of the old Horizon
Laying her spotted Face to die
Stooping as low as the Otter's Window
Touching the Roof and tinting the Barn
Kissing her Bonnet to the Meadow
And the Juggler of Day is gone

239

"Heaven" – is what I cannot reach!
The Apple on the Tree –
Provided it do hopeless – hang –
That – "Heaven" is – to Me!

The Color, on the Cruising Cloud –
The interdicted Land –
Behind the Hill – the House behind –
There – Paradise – is found!

Her teasing Purples – Afternoons –
The credulous – decoy –
Enamored – of the Conjuror –
That spurned us – Yesterday!

241

I like a look of Agony,
Because I know it's true –
Men do not sham Convulsion,
Nor simulate, a Throe –

The Eyes glaze once – and that is Death –
Impossible to feign
The Beads upon the Forehead
By homely Anguish strung.

243

I've known a Heaven, like a Tent –
To wrap its shining Yards –
Pluck up its stakes, and disappear –
Without the sound of Boards
Or Rip of Nail – Or Carpenter –
But just the miles of Stare –
That signalize a Show's Retreat –
In North America –

No Trace – no Figment of the Thing
That dazzled, Yesterday,
No Ring – no Marvel –
Men, and Feats –
Dissolved as utterly –
As Bird's far Navigation
Discloses just a Hue –
A plash of Oars, a Gaiety –
Then swallowed up, of View.

248

Why – do they shut Me out of Heaven?
Did I sing – too loud?
But – I can say a little "Minor"
Timid as a Bird!

Wouldn't the Angels try me –
Just – once – more –
Just – see – if I troubled them –
But don't – shut the door!

Oh, if I – were the Gentleman
In the "White Robe" –
And they – were the little Hand – that knocked –
Could – I – forbid?

249

Wild Nights – Wild Nights!
Were I with thee
Wild Nights should be
Our luxury!

Futile – the Winds –
To a Heart in port –
Done with the Compass –
Done with the Chart!

Rowing in Eden –
Ah, the Sea!
Might I but moor – Tonight –
In Thee!

250

I shall keep singing!
Birds will pass me
On their way to Yellower Climes –
Each – with a Robin's expectation –
I – with my Redbreast –
And my Rhymes –

Late – when I take my place in summer –
But – I shall bring a fuller tune –
Vespers – are sweeter than Matins – Signor –
Morning – only the seed of Noon –

251

Over the fence –
Strawberries – grow –
Over the fence –
I could climb – if I tried, I know –
Berries are nice!

But – if I stained my Apron –
God would certainly scold!
Oh, dear, – I guess if He were a Boy –
He'd – climb – if He could!

252

I can wade Grief –
Whole Pools of it –
I'm used to that –
But the least push of Joy
Breaks up my feet –
And I tip – drunken –
Let no Pebble – smile –
'Twas the New Liquor –
That was all!

Power is only Pain –
Stranded, thro' Discipline,
Till Weights – will hang –
Give Balm – to Giants –
And they'll wilt, like Men –
Give Himmaleh –
They'll Carry – Him!

254

"Hope" is the thing with feathers –
That perches in the soul –
And sings the tune without the words –
And never stops – at all –

And sweetest – in the Gale – is heard –
And sore must be the storm –
That could abash the little Bird
That kept so many warm –

I've heard it in the chillest land –
And on the strangest Sea –
Yet, never, in Extremity,
It asked a crumb – of Me.

258

There's a certain Slant of light,
Winter Afternoons –
That oppresses, like the Heft
Of Cathedral Tunes –

Heavenly Hurt, it gives us –
We can find no scar,
But internal difference,
Where the Meanings, are –

None may teach it – Any –
'Tis the Seal Despair –
An imperial affliction
Sent us of the Air –

When it comes, the Landscape listens –
Shadows – hold their breath –
When it goes, 'tis like the Distance
On the look of Death –

271

A solemn thing – it was – I said –
A woman – white – to be –
And wear – if God should count me fit –
Her blameless mystery –

A hallowed thing – to drop a life
Into the purple well –
Too plummetless – that it return –
Eternity – until –

I pondered how the bliss would look –
And would it feel as big –
When I could take it in my hand –
As hovering – seen – through fog –

And then – the size of this "small" life –
The Sages – call it small –
Swelled – like Horizons – in my vest –
And I sneered – softly – "small"!

273

He put the Belt around my life –
I heard the Buckle snap –
And turned away, imperial,
My Lifetime folding up –
Deliberate, as a Duke would do
A Kingdom's Title Deed –
Henceforth, a Dedicated sort –
A Member of the Cloud.

Yet not too far to come at call –
And do the little Toils
That make the Circuit of the Rest –
And deal occasional smiles
To lives that stoop to notice mine –
And kindly ask it in –
Whose invitation, know you not
For Whom I must decline?

274

The only Ghost I ever saw
Was dressed in Mechlin – so –
He wore no sandal on his foot –
And stepped like flakes of snow –

His Gait – was soundless, like the Bird –
But rapid – like the Roe –
His fashions, quaint, Mosaic –
Or haply, Mistletoe –

His conversation – seldom –
His laughter, like the Breeze –
That dies away in Dimples
Among the pensive Trees –

Our interview – was transient –
Of me, himself was shy –
And God forbid I look behind –
Since that appalling Day!

280

I felt a Funeral, in my Brain,
And Mourners to and fro
Kept treading – treading – till it seemed
That Sense was breaking through –

And when they all were seated,
A Service, like a Drum –
Kept beating – beating – till I thought
My Mind was going numb –

And then I heard them lift a Box
And creak across my Soul
With those same Boots of Lead, again,
Then Space — began to toll,

As all the Heavens were a Bell,
And Being, but an Ear,
And I, and Silence, some strange Race
Wrecked, solitary, here —

And then a Plank in Reason, broke,
And I dropped down, and down —
And hit a World, at every plunge,
And Finished knowing — then —

285

The Robin's my Criterion for Tune —
Because I grow — where Robins do —
But, were I Cuckoo born —
I'd swear by him —
The ode familiar — rules the Noon —
The Buttercup's, my Whim for Bloom —
Because, we're Orchard sprung —
But, were I Britain born,
I'd Daisies spurn —
None but the Nut — October fit —
Because, through dropping it,
The Seasons flit — I'm taught —
Without the Snow's Tableau
Winter, were lie — to me —
Because I see — New Englandly —
The Queen, discerns like me —
Provincially —

288

I'm Nobody! Who are you?
Are you – Nobody – Too?
Then there's a pair of us?
Don't tell! they'd advertise – you know!

How dreary – to be – Somebody!
How public – like a Frog –
To tell one's name – the livelong June –
To an admiring Bog!

291

How the old Mountains drip with Sunset
How the Hemlocks burn –
How the Dun Brake is draped in Cinder
By the Wizard Sun –

How the old Steeples hand the Scarlet
Till the Ball is full –
Have I the lip of the Flamingo
That I dare to tell?

Then, how the Fire ebbs like Billows –
Touching all the Grass
With a departing – Sapphire – feature –
As a Duchess passed –

How a small Dusk crawls on the Village
Till the Houses blot
And the odd Flambeau, no men carry
Glimmer on the Street –

How it is Night – in Nest and Kennel –
And where was the Wood –
Just a Dome of Abyss is Bowing
Into Solitude –

These are the Visions flitted Guido –
Titian – never told –
Domenichino dropped his pencil –
Paralyzed, with Gold –

303

The Soul selects her own Society –
Then – shuts the Door –
To her divine Majority –
Present no more –

Unmoved – she notes the Chariots – pausing –
At her low Gate –
Unmoved – an Emperor be kneeling
Upon her Mat –

I've known her – from an ample nation –
Choose One –
Then – close the Valves of her attention –
Like Stone –

311

It sifts from Leaden Sieves –
It powders all the Wood.
It fills with Alabaster Wool
The Wrinkles of the Road –

It makes an Even Face
Of Mountain, and of Plain –
Unbroken Forehead from the East
Unto the East again –

It reaches to the Fence –
It wraps it Rail by Rail
Till it is lost in Fleeces –
It flings a Crystal Vail

On Stump – and Stack – and Stem –
A Summer's empty Room –
Acres of Joints – where Harvests were,
Recordless but for them –

It Ruffles Wrists of Posts
As Ankles of a Queen –
Then stills its Artisans – like Ghosts –
Denying they have been –

312

Her – "last Poems" –
Poets – ended –
Silver – perished – with her Tongue –
Not on Record – bubbled other,
Flute – or Woman –
So divine –
Not unto its Summer – Morning
Robin – uttered Half the Tune –
Gushed too free for the Adoring –
From the Anglo-Florentine –
Late – the Praise –
'Tis dull – conferring

On the Head too High to Crown –
Diadem – or Ducal Showing –
Be its Grave – sufficient sign –
Nought – that We – No Poet's Kinsman –
Suffocate – with easy woe –
What, and if, Ourself a Bridegroom –
Put Her down – in Italy?

315

He fumbles at your Soul
As Players at the Keys
Before they drop full Music on –
He stuns you by degrees –
Prepares your brittle Nature
For the Ethereal Blow
By fainter Hammers – further heard –
Then nearer – Then so slow
Your Breath has time to straighten –
Your Brain – to bubble Cool –
Deals – One – imperial – Thunderbolt –
That scalps your naked Soul –

When Winds take Forests in their Paws –
The Universe – is still –

320

We play at Paste –
Till qualified, for Pearl –
Then, drop the Paste –
And deem ourself a fool –

The Shapes — though — were similar —
And our new Hands
Learned *Gem-Tactics* —
Practicing *Sands* —

322

There came a Day at Summer's full,
Entirely for me —
I thought that such were for the Saints,
Where Resurrections — be —

The Sun, as common, went abroad,
The flowers, accustomed, blew,
As if no soul the solstice passed
That maketh all things new —

The time was scarce profaned, by speech —
The symbol of a word
Was needless, as at Sacrament,
The Wardrobe — of our Lord —

Each was to each The Sealed Church,
Permitted to commune this — time —
Lest we too awkward show
At Supper of the Lamb.

The Hours slid fast — as Hours will,
Clutched tight, by greedy hands —
So faces on two Decks, look back,
Bound to opposing lands —

And so when all the time had leaked,
Without external sound
Each bound the Other's Crucifix —
We gave no other Bond —

Sufficient troth, that we shall rise –
Deposed – at length, the Grave –
To that new Marriage,
Justified – through Calvaries of Love –

324

Some keep the Sabbath going to Church –
I keep it, staying at Home –
With a Bobolink for a Chorister –
And an Orchard, for a Dome –

Some keep the Sabbath in Surplice –
I just wear my Wings –
And instead of tolling the Bell, for Church,
Our little Sexton – sings.

God preaches, a noted Clergyman –
And the sermon is never long,
So instead of getting to Heaven, at last –
I'm going, all along.

326

I cannot dance upon my Toes –
No Man instructed me –
But oftentimes, among my mind,
A Glee possesseth me,

That had I Ballet knowledge –
Would put itself abroad
In Pirouette to blanch a Troupe –
Or lay a Prima, mad,

And though I had no Gown of Gauze –
No Ringlet, to my Hair,
Nor hopped to Audiences – like Birds,
One Claw upon the Air,

Nor tossed my shape in Eider Balls,
Nor rolled on wheels of snow
Till I was out of sight, in sound,
The House encore me so –

Nor any know I know the Art
I mention – easy – Here –
Nor any Placard boast me –
It's full as Opera –

327

Before I got my eye put out
I liked as well to see –
As other Creatures, that have Eyes
And know no other way –

But were it told to me – Today –
That I might have the sky
For mine – I tell you that my Heart
Would split, for size of me –

The Meadows – mine –
The Mountains – mine –
All Forests – Stintless Stars –
As much of Noon as I could take
Between my finite eyes –

The Motions of the Dipping Birds –
The Morning's Amber Road –
For mine – to look at when I liked –
The News would strike me dead –

So safer – guess – with just my soul
Upon the Window pane –
Where other Creatures put their eyes –
Incautious – of the Sun –

338

I know that He exists.
Somewhere – in Silence –
He has hid his rare life
From our gross eyes.

'Tis an instant's play.
'Tis a fond Ambush –
Just to make Bliss
Earn her own surprise!

But – should the play
Prove piercing earnest –
Should the glee – glaze –
In Death's – stiff – stare –

Would not the fun
Look too expensive!
Would not the jest –
Have crawled too far!

341

After great pain, a formal feeling comes –
The Nerves sit ceremonious, like Tombs –
The stiff Heart questions was it He, that bore,
And Yesterday, or Centuries before?

The Feet, mechanical, go round –
Of Ground, or Air, or Ought –
A Wooden way
Regardless grown,
A Quartz contentment, like a stone –

This is the Hour of Lead –
Remembered, if outlived,
As Freezing persons, recollect the Snow –
First – Chill – then Stupor – then the letting go –

365

Dare you see a Soul *at the White Heat?*
Then crouch within the door –
Red – is the Fire's common tint –
But when the vivid Ore
Has vanquished Flame's conditions,
It quivers from the Forge
Without a color, but the light
Of unanointed Blaze.
Least Village has its Blacksmith
Whose Anvil's even ring
Stands symbol for the finer Forge
That soundless tugs – within –
Refining these impatient Ores
With Hammer, and with Blaze

Until the Designated Light
Repudiate the Forge –

374

I went to Heaven –
'Twas a small Town –
Lit – with a Ruby –
Lathed – with Down –

Stiller – than the fields
At the full Dew –
Beautiful – as Pictures –
No Man drew.
People – like the Moth –
Of Mechlin – frames –
Duties – of Gossamer –
And Eider – names –
Almost – contented –
I – could be –
'Mong such unique
Society –

378

I saw no Way – The Heavens were stitched –
I felt the Columns close –
The Earth reversed her Hemispheres –
I touched the Universe –

And back it slid – and I alone –
A Speck upon a Ball –
Went out upon Circumference –
Beyond the Dip of Bell –

389

There's been a Death, in the Opposite House,
As lately as Today –
I know it, by the numb look
Such Houses have – alway –

The Neighbors rustle in and out –
The Doctor – drives away –
A Window opens like a Pod –
Abrupt – mechanically –

Somebody flings a Mattress out –
The Children hurry by –
They wonder if it died – on that –
I used to – when a Boy –

The Minister – goes stiffly in –
As if the House were His –
And He owned all the Mourners – now –
And little Boys – besides –

And then the Milliner – and the Man
Of the Appalling Trade –
To take the measure of the House –

There'll be that Dark Parade –

Of Tassels – and of Coaches – soon –
It's easy as a Sign –
The Intuition of the News –
In just a Country Town –

391

A Visitor in Marl –
Who influences Flowers –
Till they are orderly as Busts –
And Elegant – as Glass –

Who visits in the Night –
And just before the Sun –
Concludes his glistening interview –
Caresses – and is gone –

But whom his fingers touched –
And where his feet have run –
And whatsoever Mouth he kissed –
Is as it had not been –

401

What Soft – Cherubic Creatures –
These Gentlewomen are –
One would as soon assault a Plush –
Or violate a Star –

Such Dimity Convictions –
A Horror so refined
Of freckled Human Nature –
Of Deity – ashamed –

It's such a common – Glory –
A Fisherman's – Degree –
Redemption – Brittle Lady –
Be so – ashamed of Thee –

414

'Twas like a Maelstrom, with a notch,
That nearer, every Day,
Kept narrowing its boiling Wheel
Until the Agony

Toyed coolly with the final inch
Of your delirious Hem —
And you dropt, lost,
When something broke —
And let you from a Dream —

As if a Goblin with a Gauge —
Kept measuring the Hours —
Until you felt your Second
Weigh, helpless, in his Paws —

And not a Sinew — stirred — could help,
And sense was setting numb —
When God — remembered — and the Fiend
Let go, then, Overcome —

As if your Sentence stood — pronounced —
And you were frozen led
From Dungeon's luxury of Doubt
To Gibbets, and the Dead —

And when the Film had stitched your eyes
A Creature gasped "Reprieve"!
Which Anguish was the utterest — then —
To perish, or to live?

425

Good Morning – Midnight –
I'm coming Home –
Day – got tired of Me –
How could I – of Him?

Sunshine was a sweet place –
I liked to stay –
But Morn – didn't want me – now –
So – Goodnight – Day!

I can look – can't I –
When the East is Red?
The Hills – have a way – then –
That puts the Heart – abroad –

You – are not so fair – Midnight –
I chose – Day –
But – please take a little Girl –
He turned away!

435

Much Madness is divinest Sense –
To a discerning Eye –
Much Sense – the starkest Madness –
'Tis the Majority
In this, as All, prevail –
Assent – and you are sane –
Demur – you're straightway dangerous –
And handled with a Chain –

441

This is my letter to the World
That never wrote to Me —
The simple News that Nature told —
With tender Majesty

Her Message is committed
To Hands I cannot see —
For love of Her — Sweet — countrymen —
Judge tenderly — of Me

448

This was a Poet — It is That
Distills amazing sense
From ordinary Meanings —
And Attar so immense

From the familiar species
That perished by the Door —
We wonder it was not Ourselves
Arrested it — before —

Of Pictures, the Discloser —
The Poet — it is He —
Entitles Us — by Contrast —
To ceaseless Poverty —

Of Portion — so unconscious —
The Robbing — could not harm —
Himself — to Him — a Fortune —
Exterior — to Time —

449

I died for Beauty – but was scarce
Adjusted in the Tomb
When One who died for Truth, was lain
In an adjoining Room –

He questioned softly "Why I failed"?
"For Beauty", I replied –
"And I – for Truth – Themself are One –
We Brethren, are", He said –

And so, as Kinsmen, met a Night –
We talked between the Rooms –
Until the Moss had reached our lips –
And covered up – our names –

451

The Outer – from the Inner
Derives its Magnitude –
'Tis Duke, or Dwarf, according
As is the Central Mood –

The fine – unvarying Axis
That regulates the Wheel –
Though Spokes – spin – more conspicuous
And fling a dust – the while.

The Inner paints the Outer –
The Brush without the Hand –
Its Picture publishes – precise –
As is the inner Brand

On fine – Arterial Canvas –
A Cheek – perchance a Brow –
The Star's whole Secret – in the Lake –
Eyes were not meant to know.

454

It was given to me by the Gods –
When I was a little Girl –
They give us Presents most – you know –
When we are new – and small.
I kept it in my Hand –
I never put it down –
I did not care to eat – or sleep –
For fear it would be gone –
I heard such words as "Rich" –
When hurrying to school –
From lips at Corners of the Streets –
And wrestled with a smile.
Rich! 'Twas Myself – was rich –
To take the name of Gold –
And Gold to own – in solid Bars –
The Difference – made me bold –

462

Why make it doubt – it hurts it so –
So sick – to guess –
So strong – to know –
So brave – upon its little Bed
To tell the very last They said

Unto Itself – and smile – And shake –
For that dear – distant – dangerous – Sake –
But – the Instead – the Pinching fear
That Something – it did do – or dare –
Offend the Vision – and it flee –
And They no more remember me –
Nor ever turn to tell me why –
Oh, Master, This is Misery –

465

I heard a Fly buzz – when I died –
The Stillness in the Room
Was like the Stillness in the Air –
Between the Heaves of Storm –

The Eyes around – had wrung them dry –
And Breaths were gathering firm
For that last Onset – when the King
Be witnessed – in the Room –

I willed my Keepsakes – Signed away
What portion of me be
Assignable – and then it was
There interposed a Fly –

With Blue – uncertain stumbling Buzz –
Between the light – and me –
And then the Windows failed – and then
I could not see to see –

475

Doom is the House without the Door —
'Tis entered from the Sun —
And then the Ladder's thrown away,
Because Escape — is done —

'Tis varied by the Dream
Of what they do outside —
Where Squirrels play — and Berries die —
And Hemlocks — bow — to God —

479

She dealt her pretty words like Blades —
How glittering they shone —
And every One unbared a Nerve
Or wantoned with a Bone —

She never deemed — she hurt —
That — is not Steel's Affair —
A vulgar grimace in the Flesh —
How ill the Creatures bear —

To Ache is human — not polite —
The Film upon the eye
Mortality's old Custom —
Just locking up — to Die.

486

I was the slightest in the House –
I took the smallest Room –
At night, my little Lamp, and Book –
And one Geranium –

So stationed I could catch the Mint
That never ceased to fall –
And just my Basket –
Let me think – I'm sure
That this was all –

I never spoke – unless addressed –
And then, 'twas brief and low –
I could not bear to live – aloud –
The Racket shamed me so –

And if it had not been so far –
And any one I knew
Were going – I had often thought
How noteless – I could die –

489

We pray – to Heaven –
We prate – of Heaven –
Relate – when Neighbors die –
At what o'clock to Heaven – they fled –
Who saw them – Wherefore fly?

Is Heaven a Place – a Sky – a Tree?
Location's narrow way is for Ourselves –
Unto the Dead
There's no Geography –

But State — Endowal — Focus —
Where — Omnipresence — fly?

492

Civilization — spurns — the Leopard!
Was the Leopard — bold?
Deserts — never rebuked her Satin —
Ethiop — her Gold —
Tawny — her Customs —
She was Conscious —
Spotted — her Dun Gown —
This was the Leopard's nature — Signor —
Need — a keeper — frown?

Pity — the Pard — that left her Asia —
Memories — of Palm —
Cannot be stifled — with Narcotic —
Nor suppressed — with Balm —

501

This World is not Conclusion.
A Species stands beyond —
Invisible, as Music —
But positive, as Sound —
It beckons, and it baffles —
Philosophy — don't know —
And through a Riddle, at the last —
Sagacity, must go —
To guess it, puzzles scholars —
To gain it, Men have borne

Contempt of Generations
And Crucifixion, shown –
Faith slips – and laughs, and rallies –
Blushes, if any see –
Plucks at a twig of Evidence –
And asks a Vane, the way –
Much Gesture, from the Pulpit –
Strong Hallelujahs roll –
Narcotics cannot still the Tooth
That nibbles at the soul –

Fascicle 17

348

I dreaded that first Robin, so,
But He is mastered, now,
I'm some accustomed to Him grown,
He hurts a little, though —

I thought if I could only live
Till that first Shout got by —
Not all Pianos in the Woods
Had power to mangle me —

I dared not meet the Daffodils —
For fear their Yellow Gown
Would pierce me with a fashion
So foreign to my own —

I wished the Grass would hurry —
So — when 'twas time to see —
He'd be too tall, the tallest one
Could stretch — to look at me —

I could not bear the Bees should come,
I wished they'd stay away
In those dim countries where they go,
What word had they, for me?

They're here, though; not a creature failed —
No Blossom stayed away
In gentle deference to me —
The Queen of Calvary —

Each one salutes me, as he goes,
And I, my childish Plumes,
Lift, in bereaved acknowledgment
Of their unthinking Drums –

505

I would not paint – a picture –
I'd rather be the One
Its bright impossibility
To dwell – delicious – on –
And wonder how the fingers feel
Whose rare – celestial – stir –
Evokes so sweet a Torment –
Such sumptuous – Despair –

I would not talk, like Cornets –
I'd rather be the One
Raised softly to the Ceilings –
And out, and easy on –
Through Villages of Ether –
Myself endued Balloon
By but a lip of Metal –
The pier to my Pontoon –

Nor would I be a Poet –
It's finer – own the Ear –
Enamored – impotent – content –
The License to revere,
A privilege so awful
What would the Dower be,
Had I the Art to stun myself
With Bolts of Melody!

506

He touched me, so I live to know
That such a day, permitted so,
I groped upon his breast –
It was a boundless place to me
And silenced, as the awful sea
Puts minor streams to rest.

And now, I'm different from before,
As if I breathed superior air –
Or brushed a Royal Gown –
My feet, too, that had wandered so –
My Gypsy face – transfigured now –
To tenderer Renown –

Into this Port, if I might come,
Rebecca, to Jerusalem,
Would not so ravished turn –
Nor Persian, baffled at her shrine
Lift such a Crucifixal sign
To her imperial Sun.

349

I had the Glory – that will do –
An Honor, Thought can turn her to
When lesser Fames invite –
With one long "Nay" –
Bliss' early shape
Deforming – Dwindling – Gulfing up –
Time's possibility.

507

She sights a Bird – she chuckles –
She flattens – then she crawls –
She runs without the look of feet –
Her eyes increase to Balls –

Her Jaws stir – twitching – hungry –
Her Teeth can hardly stand –
She leaps, but Robin leaped the first –
Ah, Pussy, of the Sand,

The Hopes so juicy ripening –
You almost bathed your Tongue –
When Bliss disclosed a hundred Toes –
And fled with every one –

350

They leave us with the Infinite.
But He – is not a man –
His fingers are the size of fists –
His fists, the size of men –

And whom he foundeth, with his Arm
As Himmaleh, shall stand –
Gibraltar's Everlasting Shoe
Poised lightly on his Hand,

So trust him, Comrade –
You for you, and I, for you and me
Eternity is ample,
And quick enough, if true.

508

I'm ceded – I've stopped being Theirs –
The name They dropped upon my face
With water, in the country church
Is finished using, now,
And They can put it with my Dolls,
My childhood, and the string of spools,
I've finished threading – too –

Baptized, before, without the choice,
But this time, consciously, of Grace –
Unto supremest name –
Called to my Full – The Crescent dropped –
Existence's whole Arc, filled up,
With one small Diadem.

My second Rank – too small the first –
Crowned – Crowing – on my Father's breast –
A half unconscious Queen –
But this time – Adequate – Erect,
With Will to choose, or to reject,
And I choose, just a Crown –

509

If anybody's friend be dead
It's sharpest of the theme
The thinking how they walked alive –
At such and such a time –

Their costume, of a Sunday,
Some manner of the Hair –
A prank nobody knew but them
Lost, in the Sepulchre –

How warm, they were, on such a day,
You almost feel the date –
So short way off it seems –
And now – they're Centuries from that –

How pleased they were, at what you said –
You try to touch the smile
And dip your fingers in the frost –
When was it – Can you tell –

You asked the Company to tea –
Acquaintance – just a few –
And chatted close with this Grand Thing
That don't remember you –

Past Bows, and Invitations –
Past Interview, and Vow –
Past what Ourself can estimate –
That – makes the Quick of Woe!

510

It was not Death, for I stood up,
And all the Dead, lie down –
It was not Night, for all the Bells
Put out their Tongues, for Noon.

It was not Frost, for on my Flesh
I felt Siroccos – crawl –
Nor Fire – for just my Marble feet
Could keep a Chancel, cool –

And yet, it tasted, like them all,
The Figures I have seen
Set orderly, for Burial,
Reminded me, of mine –

As if my life were shaven,
And fitted to a frame,
And could not breathe without a key,
And 'twas like Midnight, some –

When everything that ticked – has stopped –
And Space stares all around –
Or Grisly frosts – first Autumn morns,
Repeal the Beating Ground –

But, most, like Chaos – Stopless – cool –
Without a Chance, or Spar –
Or even a Report of Land –
To justify – Despair.

511

If you were coming in the Fall,
I'd brush the Summer by
With half a smile, and half a spurn,
As Housewives do, a Fly.

If I could see you in a year,
I'd wind the months in balls –
And put them each in separate Drawers,
For fear the numbers fuse –

If only Centuries, delayed,
I'd count them on my Hand,
Subtracting, till my fingers dropped
Into Van Dieman's Land.

If certain, when this life was out –
That yours and mine, should be
I'd toss it yonder, like a Rind,
And take Eternity –

But, now, uncertain of the length
Of this, that is between,
It goads me, like the Goblin Bee –
That will not state – its sting.

351

I felt my life with both my hands
To see if it was there –
I held my spirit to the Glass,
To prove it possibler –

I turned my Being round and round
And paused at every pound
To ask the Owner's name –
For doubt, that I should know the Sound –

I judged my features – jarred my hair –
I pushed my dimples by, and waited –
If they – twinkled back –
Conviction might, of me –

I told myself, "Take Courage, Friend –
That – was a former time –
But we might learn to like the Heaven,
As well as our Old Home!"

352

Perhaps I asked too large –
I take – no less than skies –
For Earths, grow thick as
Berries, in my native town –

My Basket holds – just – Firmaments –
Those – dangle easy – on my arm,
But smaller bundles – Cram.

328

A Bird, came down the Walk –
He did not know I saw –
He bit an Angleworm in halves
And ate the fellow, raw,

And then, he drank a Dew
From a convenient Grass –
And then hopped sidewise to the Wall
To let a Beetle pass –

He glanced with rapid eyes
That hurried all around –
They looked like frightened Beads, I thought –
He stirred his Velvet Head

Like one in danger, Cautious,
I offered him a Crumb
And he unrolled his feathers
And rowed him softer home –

Than Oars divide the Ocean,
Too silver for a seam —
Or Butterflies, off Banks of Noon
Leap, plashless as they swim.

512

The Soul has Bandaged moments —
When too appalled to stir —
She feels some ghastly Fright come up
And stop to look at her —

Salute her — with long fingers —
Caress her freezing hair —
Sip, Goblin, from the very lips
The Lover — hovered — o'er —
Unworthy, that a thought so mean
Accost a Theme — so — fair —

The soul has moments of Escape —
When bursting all the doors —
She dances like a Bomb, abroad,
And swings upon the Hours,

As do the Bee — delirious borne —
Long Dungeoned from his Rose —
Touch liberty — then know no more,
But Noon, and Paradise —

The Soul's retaken moments —
When, Felon led along,
With shackles on the plumed feet,
And staples, in the Song,

The Horror welcomes her, again,
These, are not brayed of Tongue —

513

Like Flowers, that heard the news of Dews,
But never deemed the dripping prize
Awaited their — low Brows —

Or Bees — that thought the Summer's name
Some rumour of Delirium,
No Summer — could — for Them —

Or Arctic Creatures, dimly stirred —
By Tropic Hint — some Travelled Bird
Imported to the Word —

Or Wind's bright signal to the Ear —
Making that homely, and severe,
Contented, known, before —

The Heaven — unexpected come,
To Lives that thought the Worshipping
A too presumptuous Psalm —

END OF FASCICLE 17

518

Her sweet Weight on my Heart a Night
Had scarcely deigned to lie —
When, stirring, for Belief's delight,
My Bride had slipped away —

If 'twas a Dream – made solid – just
The Heaven to confirm –
Or if Myself were dreamed of Her –
The power to presume –

With Him remain – who unto Me –
Gave – even as to All –
A Fiction superseding Faith –
By so much – as 'twas real –

520

I started Early – Took my Dog –
And visited the Sea –
The Mermaids in the Basement
Came out to look at me –

And Frigates – in the Upper Floor
Extended Hempen Hands –
Presuming Me to be a Mouse –
Aground – upon the Sands –

But no Man moved Me – till the Tide
Went past my simple Shoe –
And past my Apron – and my Belt
And past my Bodice – too –

And made as He would eat me up –
As wholly as a Dew
Upon a Dandelion's Sleeve –
And then – I started – too –

And He – He followed – close behind –
I felt his Silver Heel
Upon my Ankle – Then my Shoes
Would overflow with Pearl –

Until We met the Solid Town –
No One He seemed to know –
And bowing – with a Mighty look –
At me – The Sea withdrew –

528

Mine – by the Right of the White Election!
Mine – by the Royal Seal!
Mine – by the Sign in the Scarlet prison –
Bars – cannot conceal!

Mine – here – in Vision – and in Veto!
Mine – by the Grave's Repeal –
Titled – Confirmed –
Delirious Charter!
Mine – long as Ages steal!

536

The Heart asks Pleasure – first –
And then – Excuse from Pain –
And then – those little Anodynes
That deaden suffering –

And then – to go to sleep –
And then – if it should be
The will of its Inquisitor
The privilege to die –

544

The Martyr Poets – did not tell –
But wrought their Pang in syllable –
That when their mortal name be numb –
Their mortal fate – encourage Some –
The Martyr Painters – never spoke –
Bequeathing – rather – to their Work –
That when their conscious fingers cease –
Some seek in Art – the Art of Peace –

546

To fill a Gap
Insert the Thing that caused it –
Block it up
With Other – and 'twill yawn the more –
You cannot solder an Abyss
With Air.

547

I've seen a Dying Eye
Run round and round a Room –
In search of Something – as it seemed –
Then Cloudier become –
And then – obscure with Fog –
And then – be soldered down
Without disclosing what it be
'Twere blessed to have seen –

569

I reckon – when I count at all –
First – Poets – Then the Sun –
Then Summer – Then the Heaven of God –
And then – the List is done –

But, looking back – the First so seems
To Comprehend the Whole –
The Others look a needless Show –
So I write – Poets – All –

Their Summer – lasts a Solid Year –
They can afford a Sun
The East – would deem extravagant –
And if the Further Heaven –

Be Beautiful as they prepare
For Those who worship Them –
It is too difficult a Grace –
To justify the Dream –

570

I could die – to know –
'Tis a trifling knowledge –
News-Boys salute the Door –
Carts – joggle by –
Morning's bold face – stares in the window –
Were but mine – the Charter of the least Fly –

Houses hunch the House
With their Brick Shoulders –
Coals – from a Rolling Load – rattle – how – near –
To the very Square – His foot is passing –
Possibly, this moment –
While I – dream – Here –

572

Delight – becomes pictorial –
When viewed through Pain –
More fair – because impossible
That any gain –

The Mountain – at a given distance –
In Amber – lies –
Approached – the Amber flits – a little –
And That's – the Skies –

575

"Heaven" has different Signs – to me –
Sometimes, I think that Noon
Is but a symbol of the Place –
And when again, at Dawn,

A mighty look runs round the World
And settles in the Hills –
An Awe if it should be like that
Upon the Ignorance steals –

The Orchard, when the Sun is on –
The Triumph of the Birds
When they together Victory make –
Some Carnivals of Clouds –

The Rapture of a finished Day –
Returning to the West –
All these – remind us of the place
That Men call "Paradise" –

Itself be fairer – we suppose –
But how Ourself, shall be
Adorned, for a Superior Grace –
Not yet, our eyes can see –

581

I found the words to every thought
I ever had – but One –
And that – defies me –
As a Hand did try to chalk the Sun

To Races – nurtured in the Dark –
How would your own – begin?
Can Blaze be shown in Cochineal –
Or Noon – in Mazarin?

585

I like to see it lap the Miles –
And lick the Valleys up –
And stop to feed itself at Tanks –
And then – prodigious step

Around a Pile of Mountains –
And supercilious peer
In Shanties – by the sides of Roads –
And then a Quarry pare

To fit its Ribs
And crawl between
Complaining all the while
In horrid – hooting stanza –
Then chase itself down Hill –

And neigh like Boanerges –
Then – punctual as a Star
Stop – docile and omnipotent
At its own stable door –

587

Empty my Heart, of Thee –
Its single Artery –
Begin, and leave Thee out –
Simply Extinction's Date –

Much Billow hath the Sea –
On Baltic – They –
Subtract Thyself, in play,
And not enough of me
Is left – to put away –
"Myself" meant Thee –

Erase the Root – no Tree –
Thee – then – no me –
The Heavens stripped –
Eternity's vast pocket, picked –

593

I think I was enchanted
When first a sombre Girl —
I read that Foreign Lady —
The Dark — felt beautiful —

And whether it was noon at night —
Or only Heaven — at Noon —
For very Lunacy of Light
I had not power to tell —

The Bees — became as Butterflies —
The Butterflies — as Swans
Approached — and spurned the narrow Grass —
And just the meanest Tunes

That Nature murmured to herself
To keep herself in Cheer —
I took for Giants — practising
Titanic Opera —

The Days — to Mighty Metres stept —
The Homeliest — adorned
As if unto a Jubilee
'Twere suddenly confirmed —

I could not have defined the change —
Conversion of the Mind
Like Sanctifying in the Soul —
Is witnessed — not explained —

'Twas a Divine Insanity
The Danger to be Sane
Should I again experience —
'Tis Antidote to turn —

To Tomes of solid Witchcraft –
Magicians be asleep –
But Magic – hath an Element
Like Deity – to keep –

599

There is a pain – so utter –
It swallows substance up –
Then covers the Abyss with Trance –
So Memory can step
Around – across – upon it –
As one within a Swoon –
Goes safely – where an open eye –
Would drop Him – Bone by Bone.

601

A still – Volcano – Life –
That flickered in the night –
When it was dark enough to do
Without erasing sight –

A quiet – Earthquake Style –
Too subtle to suspect
By natures this side Naples –
The North cannot detect

The Solemn – Torrid – Symbol –
The lips that never lie –
Whose hissing Corals part – and shut –
And Cities – ooze away –

606

The Trees like Tassels – hit – and swung –
There seemed to rise a Tune
From Miniature Creatures
Accompanying the Sun –

Far Psalteries of Summer –
Enamoring the Ear
They never yet did satisfy –
Remotest – when most fair

The Sun shone whole at intervals –
Then Half – then utter hid –
As if Himself were optional
And had Estates of Cloud

Sufficient to enfold Him
Eternally from view –
Except it were a whim of His
To let the Orchards grow –

A Bird sat careless on the fence –
One gossipped in the Lane
On silver matters charmed a Snake
Just winding round a Stone –

Bright Flowers slit a Calyx
And soared upon a Stem
Like Hindered Flags – Sweet hoisted –
With Spices – in the Hem –

'Twas more – I cannot mention –
How mean – to those that see –
Vandyke's Delineation
Of Nature's – Summer Day!

607

Of nearness to her sundered Things
The Soul has special times –
When Dimness – looks the Oddity –
Distinctness – easy – seems –

The Shapes we buried, dwell about,
Familiar, in the Rooms –
Untarnished by the Sepulchre,
The Mouldering Playmate comes –

In just the Jacket that he wore –
Long buttoned in the Mold
Since we – old mornings, Children – played –
Divided – by a world –

The Grave yields back her Robberies –
The Years, our pilfered Things –
Bright Knots of Apparitions
Salute us, with their wings –

As we – it were – that perished –
Themself – had just remained till we rejoin them –
And 'twas they, and not ourself
That mourned.

613

They shut me up in Prose –
As when a little Girl
They put me in the Closet –
Because they liked me "still" –

Still! Could themself have peeped —
And seen my Brain — go round —
They might as wise have lodged a Bird
For Treason — in the Pound —

Himself has but to will
And easy as a Star
Abolish his Captivity —
And laugh — No more have I —

617

Don't put up my Thread and Needle —
I'll begin to Sew
When the Birds begin to whistle —
Better Stitches — so —

These were bent — my sight got crooked —
When my mind — is plain
I'll do seams — a Queen's endeavor
Would not blush to own —

Hems — too fine for Lady's tracing
To the sightless Knot —
Tucks — of dainty interspersion —
Like a dotted Dot —

Leave my Needle in the furrow —
Where I put it down —
I can make the zigzag stitches
Straight — when I am strong —

Till then — dreaming I am sewing
Fetch the seam I missed —
Closer — so I — at my sleeping —
Still surmise I stitch —

627

The Tint I cannot take – is best –
The Color too remote
That I could show it in Bazaar –
A Guinea at a sight –

The fine – impalpable Array –
That swaggers on the eye
Like Cleopatra's Company –
Repeated – in the sky –

The Moments of Dominion
That happen on the Soul
And leave it with a Discontent
Too exquisite – to tell –

The eager look – on Landscapes –
As if they just repressed
Some Secret – that was pushing
Like Chariots – in the Vest –

The Pleading of the Summer –
That other Prank – of Snow –
That Cushions Mystery with Tulle,
For fear the Squirrels – know.

Their Graspless manners – mock us –
Until the Cheated Eye
Shuts arrogantly – in the Grave –
Another way – to see –

640

I cannot live with You –
It would be Life –
And Life is over there –
Behind the Shelf

The Sexton keeps the Key to –
Putting up
Our Life – His Porcelain –
Like a Cup –

Discarded of the Housewife –
Quaint – or Broke –
A newer Sevres pleases –
Old Ones crack –

I could not die – with You –
For One must wait
To shut the Other's Gaze down
You – could not –

And I – Could I stand by
And see You – freeze –
Without my Right of Frost –
Death's privilege?

Nor could I rise – with You –
Because Your Face
Would put out Jesus' –
That New Grace

Glow plain – and foreign
On my homesick Eye –
Except that You than He
Shone closer by –

They'd judge Us – How –
For You – served Heaven – You know,
Or sought to –
I could not –

Because You saturated Sight –
And I had no more Eyes,
For sordid excellence
As Paradise

And were You lost, I would be –
Though My Name
Rang loudest
On the Heavenly fame –

And were You – saved –
And I – condemned to be
Where You were not –
That self – were Hell to Me –

So We must meet apart –
You there – I – here –
With just the Door ajar
That Oceans are – and Prayer –
And that White Sustenance –
Despair –

642

Me from Myself – to banish –
Had I Art –
Impregnable my Fortress
Unto All Heart –

But since Myself — assault Me —
How have I peace
Except by subjugating
Consciousness?

And since We're mutual Monarch
How this be
Except by Abdication —
Me — of Me?

646

I think to Live — may be a Bliss
To those who dare to try —
Beyond my limit to conceive —
My lip — to testify —

I think the Heart I former wore
Could widen — till to me
The Other, like the little Bank
Appear — unto the Sea —

I think the Days — could every one
In Ordination stand —
And Majesty — be easier —
Than an inferior kind —

No numb alarm — lest Difference come —
No Goblin — on the Bloom —
No start in Apprehension's Ear,
No Bankruptcy — no Doom —

But Certainties of Sun —
Midsummer — in the Mind —
A steadfast South — upon the Soul —
Her Polar time — behind —

The Vision — pondered long —
So plausible becomes
That I esteem the fiction — real —
The Real — fictitious seems —

How bountiful the Dream —
What Plenty — it would be —
Had all my Life but been Mistake
Just rectified — in Thee

650

Pain — has an Element of Blank —
It cannot recollect
When it begun — or if there were
A time when it was not —

It has no Future — but itself —
Its Infinite contain
Its Past — enlightened to perceive
New Periods — of Pain.

657

I dwell in Possibility —
A fairer House than Prose —
More numerous of Windows —
Superior — for Doors —

Of Chambers as the Cedars —
Impregnable of Eye —
And for an Everlasting Roof
The Gambrels of the Sky —

Of Visitors – the fairest –
For Occupation – This –
The spreading wide my narrow Hands
To gather Paradise –

670

One need not be a Chamber – to be Haunted –
One need not be a House –
The Brain has Corridors – surpassing
Material Place –

Far safer, of a Midnight Meeting
External Ghost
Than its interior Confronting –
That Cooler Host.

Far safer, through an Abbey gallop,
The Stones a'chase –
Than Unarmed, one's a'self encounter –
In lonesome Place –

Ourself behind ourself, concealed –
Should startle most –
Assassin hid in our Apartment
Be Horror's least.

The Body – borrows a Revolver –
He bolts the Door –
O'erlooking a superior spectre –
Or More –

675

Essential Oils – are wrung –
The Attar from the Rose
Be not expressed by Suns – alone –
It is the gift of Screws –

The General Rose – decay –
But this – in Lady's Drawer
Make Summer – When the Lady lie
In Ceaseless Rosemary –

690

Victory comes late –
And is held low to freezing lips –
Too rapt with frost
To take it –
How sweet it would have tasted –
Just a Drop –
Was God so economical?
His Table's spread too high for Us –
Unless We dine on tiptoe –
Crumbs fit such little mouths –
Cherries – suit Robins –
The Eagle's Golden Breakfast strangles – Them –
God keep His Oath to Sparrows –
Who of little Love – know how to starve –

709

Publication – is the Auction
Of the Mind of Man –
Poverty – be justifying
For so foul a thing

Possibly – but We – would rather
From Our Garret go
White – Unto the White Creator –
Than invest – Our Snow –

Thought belong to Him who gave it –
Then – to Him Who bear
Its Corporeal illustration – Sell
The Royal Air –

In the Parcel – Be the Merchant
Of the Heavenly Grace –
But reduce no Human Spirit
To Disgrace of Price –

711

Strong Draughts of Their Refreshing Minds
To drink – enables Mine
Through Desert or the Wilderness
As bore it Sealed Wine –

To go elastic – Or as One
The Camel's trait – attained –
How powerful the Stimulus
Of an Hermetic Mind –

712

Because I could not stop for Death –
He kindly stopped for me –
The Carriage held but just Ourselves –
And Immortality.

We slowly drove – He knew no haste
And I had put away
My labor and my leisure too,
For His Civility –

We passed the School, where Children strove
At Recess – in the Ring –
We passed the Fields of Gazing Grain –
We passed the Setting Sun –

Or rather – He passed Us –
The Dews drew quivering and chill –
For only Gossamer, my Gown –
My Tippet – only Tulle –

We paused before a House that seemed
A Swelling of the Ground –
The Roof was scarcely visible –
The Cornice – in the Ground –

Since then – 'tis Centuries – and yet
Feels shorter than the Day
I first surmised the Horses' Heads
Were toward Eternity –

721

Behind Me – dips Eternity –
Before Me – Immortality –
Myself – the Term between –

Death but the Drift of Eastern Gray,
Dissolving into Dawn away,
Before the West begin –

'Tis Kingdoms – afterward – they say –
In perfect – pauseless Monarchy –
Whose Prince – is Son of None –
Himself – His Dateless Dynasty –
Himself – Himself diversify –
In Duplicate divine –

'Tis Miracle before Me – then –
'Tis Miracle behind – between –
A Crescent in the Sea –
With Midnight to the North of Her –
And Midnight to the South of Her –
And Maelstrom – in the Sky –

728

Let Us play Yesterday –
I – the Girl at school –
You – and Eternity – the
Untold Tale –

Easing my famine
At my Lexicon –
Logarithm – had I – for Drink –
'Twas a dry Wine –

Somewhat different – must be –
Dreams tint the Sleep –
Cunning Reds of Morning
Make the Blind – leap –

Still at the Egg-life –
Chafing the Shell –
When you troubled the Ellipse –
And the Bird fell –

Manacles be dim – they say –
To the new Free –
Liberty – Commoner –
Never could – to me –

'Twas my last gratitude
When I slept – at night –
'Twas the first Miracle
Let in – with Light –

Can the Lark resume the Shell –
Easier – for the Sky –
Wouldn't Bonds hurt more
Than Yesterday?

Wouldn't Dungeons sorer grate
On the Man – free –
Just long enough to taste –
Then – doomed new –

God of the Manacle
As of the Free –
Take not my Liberty
Away from Me –

741

Drama's Vitallest Expression is the Common Day
That arise and set about Us —
Other Tragedy

Perish in the Recitation —
This — the best enact
When the Audience is scattered
And the Boxes shut —

"Hamlet" to Himself were Hamlet —
Had not Shakespeare wrote —
Though the "Romeo" left no Record
Of his Juliet,

It were infinite enacted
In the Human Heart —
Only Theatre recorded
Owner cannot shut —

754

My Life had stood — a Loaded Gun —
In Corners — till a Day
The Owner passed — identified —
And carried Me away —

And now We roam in Sovereign Woods —
And now We hunt the Doe —
And every time I speak for Him —
The Mountains straight reply —

And do I smile, such cordial light
Upon the Valley glow –
It is as a Vesuvian face
Had let its pleasure through –

And when at Night – Our good Day done –
I guard My Master's Head –
'Tis better than the Eider-Duck's
Deep Pillow – to have shared –

To foe of His – I'm deadly foe –
None stir the second time –
On whom I lay a Yellow Eye –
Or an emphatic Thumb –

Though I than He – may longer live
He longer must – than I –
For I have but the power to kill,
Without – the power to die –

762

The Whole of it came not at once –
'Twas Murder by degrees –
A Thrust – and then for Life a chance –
The Bliss to cauterize –

The Cat reprieves the Mouse
She eases from her teeth
Just long enough for Hope to tease –
Then mashes it to death –

'Tis Life's award – to die –
Contendeder if once –
Than dying half – then rallying
For consciouser Eclipse –

784

Bereaved of all, I went abroad —
No less bereaved was I
Upon a New Peninsula —
The Grave preceded me —

Obtained my Lodgings, ere myself —
And when I sought my Bed —
The Grave it was reposed upon
The Pillow for my Head —

I waked to find it first awake —
I rose — It followed me —
I tried to drop it in the Crowd —
To lose it in the Sea —

In Cups of artificial Drowse
To steep its shape away —
The Grave — was finished — but the Spade
Remained in Memory —

797

By my Window have I for Scenery
Just a Sea — with a Stem —
If the Bird and the Farmer — deem it a "Pine" —
The Opinion will serve — for them —

It has no Port, nor a "Line" — but the Jays —
That split their route to the Sky —
Or a Squirrel, whose giddy Peninsula
May be easier reached — this way —

For Inlands – the Earth is the under side –
And the upper side – is the Sun –
And its Commerce – if Commerce it have –
Of Spice – I infer from the Odors borne –

Of its Voice – to affirm – when the Wind is within –
Can the Dumb – define the Divine?
The Definition of Melody – is –
That Definition is none –

It – suggests to our Faith –
They – suggest to our Sight –
When the latter – is put away
I shall meet with Conviction I somewhere met
That Immortality –

Was the Pine at my Window a "Fellow
Of the Royal" Infinity?
Apprehensions – are God's introductions –
To be hallowed – accordingly –

824

The Wind begun to knead the Grass –
As Women do a Dough –
He flung a Hand full at the Plain –
A Hand full at the Sky –
The Leaves unhooked themselves from Trees –
And started all abroad –
The Dust did scoop itself like Hands –
And throw away the Road –
The Wagons quickened on the Street –
The Thunders gossiped low –
The Lightning showed a Yellow Head –
And then a livid Toe –

The Birds put up the Bars to Nests —
The Cattle flung to Barns —
Then came one drop of Giant Rain —
And then, as if the Hands
That held the Dams — had parted hold —
The Waters Wrecked the Sky —
But overlooked my Father's House —
Just Quartering a Tree —

FIRST VERSION c. 1864

The Wind begun to rock the Grass
With threatening Tunes and low —
He threw a Menace at the Earth —
A Menace at the Sky.

The Leaves unhooked themselves from Trees —
And started all abroad
The Dust did scoop itself like Hands
And threw away the Road.

The Wagons quickened on the Streets
The Thunder hurried slow —
The Lightning showed a Yellow Beak
And then a livid Claw.

The Birds put up the Bars to Nests —
The Cattle fled to Barns —
There came one drop of Giant Rain
And then as if the Hands

That held the Dams had parted hold
The Waters Wrecked the Sky,
But overlooked my Father's House —
Just quartering a Tree —

SECOND VERSION c. 1864

76

861

Split the Lark – and you'll find the Music –
Bulb after Bulb, in Silver rolled –
Scantily dealt to the Summer Morning
Saved for your Ear when Lutes be old.

Loose the Flood – you shall find it patent –
Gush after Gush, reserved for you –
Scarlet Experiment! Sceptic Thomas!
Now, do you doubt that your Bird was true?

875

I stepped from Plank to Plank
A slow and cautious way
The Stars about my Head I felt
About my Feet the Sea.

I knew not but the next
Would be my final inch –
This gave me that precarious Gait
Some call Experience.

889

Crisis is a Hair
Toward which the forces creep
Past which forces retrograde
If it come in sleep

To suspend the Breath
Is the most we can
Ignorant is it Life or Death
Nicely balancing.

Let an instant push
Or an Atom press
Or a Circle hesitate
In Circumference

It — may jolt the Hand
That adjusts the Hair
That secures Eternity
From presenting — Here —

909

I make His Crescent fill or lack —
His Nature is at Full
Or Quarter — as I signify —
His Tides — do I control —

He holds superior in the Sky
Or gropes, at my Command
Behind inferior Clouds — or round
A Mist's slow Colonnade —

But since We hold a Mutual Disc —
And front a Mutual Day —
Which is the Despot, neither knows —
Nor Whose — the Tyranny —

985

The Missing All – prevented Me
From missing minor Things.
If nothing larger than a World's
Departure from a Hinge –
Or Sun's extinction, be observed –
'Twas not so large that I
Could lift my Forehead from my work
For Curiosity.

986

A narrow Fellow in the Grass
Occasionally rides –
You may have met Him – did you not
His notice sudden is –

The Grass divides as with a Comb –
A spotted shaft is seen –
And then it closes at your feet
And opens further on –

He likes a Boggy Acre
A Floor too cool for Corn –
Yet when a Boy, and Barefoot –
I more than once at Noon
Have passed, I thought, a Whip lash
Unbraiding in the Sun
When stooping to secure it
It wrinkled, and was gone –

Several of Nature's People
I know, and they know me –
I feel for them a transport
Of cordiality –

But never met this Fellow
Attended, or alone
Without a tighter breathing
And Zero at the Bone –

1021

Far from Love the Heavenly Father
Leads the Chosen Child,
Oftener through Realm of Briar
Than the Meadow mild.

Oftener by the Claw of Dragon
Than the Hand of Friend
Guides the Little One predestined
To the Native Land.

1071

Perception of an object costs
Precise the Object's loss –
Perception in itself a Gain
Replying to its Price –

The Object Absolute – is nought –
Perception sets it fair
And then upbraids a Perfectness
That situates so far –

1072

Title divine – is mine!
The Wife – without the Sign!
Acute Degree – conferred on me –
Empress of Calvary!
Royal – all but the Crown!
Betrothed – without the swoon
God sends us Women –
When you – hold – Garnet to Garnet –
Gold – to Gold –
Born – Bridalled – Shrouded –
In a Day –
Tri Victory
"My Husband" – women say –
Stroking the Melody –
Is *this* – the way?

1129

Tell all the Truth but tell it slant –
Success in Circuit lies
Too bright for our infirm Delight
The Truth's superb surprise

As Lightning to the Children eased
With explanation kind
The Truth must dazzle gradually
Or every man be blind –

1263

There is no Frigate like a Book
To take us Lands away
Nor any Coursers like a Page
Of prancing Poetry –
This Traverse may the poorest take
Without oppress of Toll –
How frugal is the Chariot
That bears the Human soul.

1304

Not with a Club, the Heart is broken
Nor with a Stone –
A Whip so small you could not see it
I've known

To lash the Magic Creature
Till it fell,
Yet that Whip's Name
Too noble then to tell.

Magnanimous as Bird
By Boy descried –
Singing unto the Stone
Of which it died –

Shame need not crouch
In such an Earth as Ours –
Shame – stand erect –
The Universe is yours.

1311

This dirty – little – Heart
Is freely mine.
I won it with a Bun –
A Freckled shrine –

But eligibly fair
To him who sees
The Visage of the Soul
And not the knees.

1412

Shame is the shawl of Pink
In which we wrap the Soul
To keep it from infesting Eyes –
The elemental Veil
Which helpless Nature drops
When pushed upon a scene
Repugnant to her probity –
Shame is the tint divine.

1498

Glass was the Street – in tinsel Peril
Tree and Traveller stood –
Filled was the Air with merry venture
Hearty with Boys the Road –

Shot the lithe Sleds like shod vibrations
Emphasized and gone
It is the Past's supreme italic
Makes this Present mean –

1515

The Things that never can come back, are several —
Childhood — some forms of Hope — the Dead —
Though Joys — like Men — may sometimes make a
    Journey —
And still abide —
We do not mourn for Traveler, or Sailor,
Their Routes are fair —
But think enlarged of all that they will tell us
Returning here —
"Here!" There are typic "Heres" —
Foretold Locations —
The Spirit does not stand —
Himself — at whatsoever Fathom
His Native Land —

1545

The Bible is an antique Volume —
Written by faded Men
At the suggestion of Holy Spectres —
Subjects — Bethlehem —
Eden — the ancient Homestead —
Satan — the Brigadier —
Judas — the Great Defaulter —
David — the Troubadour —
Sin — a distinguished Precipice
Others must resist —
Boys that "believe" are very lonesome —
Other Boys are "lost" —
Had but the Tale a warbling Teller —

All the Boys would come –
Orpheus' Sermon captivated –
It did not condemn –

1551

Those – dying then,
Knew where they went –
They went to God's Right Hand –
That Hand is amputated now
And God cannot be found –

The abdication of Belief
Makes the Behavior small –
Better an ignis fatuus
Than no illume at all –

1562

Her Losses make our Gains ashamed –
She bore Life's empty Pack
As gallantly as if the East
Were swinging at her Back.
Life's empty Pack is heaviest,
As every Porter knows –
In vain to punish Honey –
It only sweeter grows.

1593

There came a Wind like a Bugle –
It quivered through the Grass
And a Green Chill upon the Heat
So ominous did pass
We barred the Windows and the Doors
As from an Emerald Ghost –
The Doom's electric Moccasin
That very instant passed –
On a strange Mob of panting Trees
And Fences fled away
And Rivers where the Houses ran
Those looked that lived – that Day –
The Bell within the steeple wild
The flying tidings told –
How much can come
And much can go,
And yet abide the World!

1598

Who is it seeks my Pillow Nights –
With plain inspecting face –
"Did you" or "Did you not," to ask –
'Tis "Conscience" – Childhood's Nurse –

With Martial Hand she strokes the Hair
Upon my wincing Head –
"All" Rogues "shall have their part in" what –
The Phosphorus of God –

1601

Of God we ask one favor,
That we may be forgiven –
For what, he is presumed to know –
The Crime, from us, is hidden –
Immured the whole of Life
Within a magic Prison
We reprimand the Happiness
That too competes with Heaven.

1651

A Word made Flesh is seldom
And tremblingly partook
Nor then perhaps reported
But have I not mistook
Each one of us has tasted
With ecstasies of stealth
The very food debated
To our specific strength –

A Word that breathes distinctly
Has not the power to die
Cohesive as the Spirit
It may expire if He –
"Made Flesh and dwelt among us"
Could condescension be
Like this consent of Language
This loved Philology.

1670

In Winter in my Room
I came upon a Worm —
Pink, lank and warm —
But as he was a worm
And worms presume
Not quite with him at home —
Secured him by a string
To something neighboring
And went along.

A Trifle afterward
A thing occurred
I'd not believe it if I heard
But state with creeping blood —
A snake with mottles rare
Surveyed my chamber floor
In feature as the worm before
But ringed with power —

The very string with which
I tied him — too
When he was mean and new
That string was there —

I shrank — "How fair you are"!
Propitiation's claw —
"Afraid," he hissed
"Of me"?
"No cordiality" —
He fathomed me —
Then to a Rhythm Slim
Secreted in his Form
As Patterns swim
Projected him.

That time I flew
Both eyes his way
Lest he pursue
Nor ever ceased to run
Till in a distant Town
Towns on from mine
I set me down
This was a dream.

1705

Volcanoes be in Sicily
And South America
I judge from my Geography –
Volcanoes nearer here
A Lava step at any time
Am I inclined to climb –
A Crater I may contemplate
Vesuvius at Home.

1732

My life closed twice before its close –
It yet remains to see
If Immortality unveil
A third event to me

So huge, so hopeless to conceive
As these that twice befell.
Parting is all we know of heaven,
And all we need of hell.

Chronology of Dickinson's Life

Year	Life
1830	Emily Dickinson born 10 December in Amherst, Massachusetts, USA, the second child of lawyer Edward Dickinson and Emily Norcross Dickinson
1840	Edward sells his half of the family home, The Homestead, and the family moves to another house in Amherst. Emily enters Amherst Academy, where students are taught a 'modern' curriculum including astronomy and pre-Darwinian geology
1842	Her father elected State Senator; re-elected 1843
1846	Religious revival in Amherst; Dickinson expresses doubts to her friend Abiah Root
1847	Enters Mount Holyoke Female Seminary
1848	Withdraws from Mount Holyoke
1850	Another religious revival in Amherst; her father, sister Lavinia and her friend, Susan Gilbert, join First Church of Christ
1851	Travels with her sister to Boston
1852	Her father is elected to the US House of Representatives
1855	Edward moves his family back into The Homestead; Dickinson will stay here for the rest of her life
1858	Writing poetry seriously
1861	*Springfield Republican* prints poem 'I taste a liquor never brewed', altered and titled 'The May-Wine'
1862–3	Writes about 300 poems but undergoes a personal crisis. Shares Amherst's grief for loss of men killed in the Civil War

Chronology of her Times

Year	Life
1864	In Boston for seven months for eye treatment. Two more poems printed
1865	About a thousand poems written by the end of this year
1866	*Springfield Republican* prints 'A narrow Fellow in the Grass' in a much-altered form
1876	Helen Hunt Jackson, Amherst-born poet, becomes literary friend and begs her to publish
1878	'Success is counted sweetest' published anonymously at Jackson's urging
1880	Judge Otis Lord calls frequently at The Homestead and discusses marriage but is turned down
1882	Mother Emily dies
1884	First attack of kidney disease
1886	Dies of kidney disease
1890	First selection of poetry published

Year	Literary Context	Historical Events
1863	Tolstoy, *The Cossacks*	Emancipation proclamation
		Battle of Gettysburg
1864	Death of Hawthorne	General Sherman captures Savannah
1865	Kipling and Yeats born	Civil War ends
		Lincoln assassinated
1866	Dostoevsky, *Crime and Punishment*	Fourteenth Amendment
		Transatlantic cable laid
		Ulysses S. Grant elected President
1874	Frost, Lowell and Stein born	
1876	Tolstoy, *Anna Karenina*	Bell's speaking telephone
	Twain, *Tom Sawyer*	Battle of Little Big Horn
1880	Wallace Stevens born	Boer uprising in Transvaal
1882	Death of Emerson	
1885	Twain, *Huckleberry Finn*	Grover Cleveland elected President
1886	Ezra Pound born	Completion of Canadian Pacific Railway
	James, *The Bostonians*	

This edition first published in 2010
Phoenix edition first published in 2002

Selection © J. M. Dent 1996
Chronology © J. M. Dent 2002

Typeset by Deltatype Ltd
Birkenhead, Merseyside

Printed in Great Britain by
Clays Ltd, St Ives plc

A CIP catalogue reference for this book
is available from the British Library.

The Orion Publishing Group
Orion House
5 Upper St Martin's Lane
London
WC2H 9EA

Emily Dickinson

Selected by
Helen McNeil

PHOENIX